THE AMERICAN CHURCHES
AN INTERPRETATION

THE AMERICAN CHURCHES

AN INTERPRETATION

BY

WILLIAM WARREN SWEET, Ph.D.

The University of Chicago

The Social Service Lecture, 1946

THE EPWORTH PRESS

(EDGAR C. BARTON)

25-35 CITY ROAD, LONDON, E.C.1

*Published for the Social
Service Lecture Trust*

Made in Great Britain

DEDICATED
TO
DR. WILLIAM F. LOFTHOUSE

PREFACE

THE BECKLY TRUST calls for a yearly lecture before the Conference of the Methodist Church on the social implications of Christianity with emphasis upon the Christian attitude toward social, industrial, economic, and international affairs. The principal justification for this lecture is that of all the Protestant Churches of Christendom none has given so much attention through the years to the practical application of the Christian message to society as have those of the United States. The extent to which this is true, and the reason for it, will appear, I hope, as the lecture proceeds.

I would no doubt win favour with my readers if I were able to explain the American emphasis upon the practical application of the Gospel in contemporary terms. But unfortunately that is an impossibility. Any adequate discussion of this subject must deal with its historic roots, and of necessity I must therefore call to your attention certain historic developments which have occurred in the more than three hundred years since the first American Churches began to take root in American soil. I shall not, however, attempt to deal with the history of the American Churches as such. Rather my purpose is to bring out in clear relief those historic influences which have made the American Churches what they are to-day, stressing particularly those factors and forces in their development which are distinctly American.

I should like to add a word of appreciation for the many kindnesses I have received during my short visit to England at the hands of numerous English Methodists. To Dr. W. F. Lofthouse, the Secretary of the Beckly Trust, to whom this little book is dedicated, I am especially indebted in more ways than I can enumerate here. The Rev. Edgar C. Barton, the Book Steward, and his capable staff at the Epworth Press were uniformly helpful in putting the manuscript in shape for the press and in adjusting my Americanisms to English readers.

CONTENTS

Preface vii

Chapter I. Left-Wing Protestantism triumphs in Colonial
America I

Chapter II. Religion in the Winning of the West . . 13

Chapter III. Revivalism in American Protestantism . . 22

Chapter IV. The Multiplicity of Denominations . . 28

Chapter V. The American Negro and his Religion . . 39

Chapter VI. Roman Catholicism in the United States . 45

Chapter VII. Activism in the American Tradition . . 54

Index 75

CHAPTER ONE

LEFT-WING PROTESTANTISM TRIUMPHS IN COLONIAL AMERICA

IF WE ARE to have any full understanding of the religious development of America we must start with the Reformation and the rise of Protestantism. In the early days of American independence it was the custom of Protestant ministers to speak of the discovery of America and the beginning of the Reformation as providentially contemporaneous events. It seemed to them that a divine wisdom and a controlling providence had kept the very existence of America a secret until Protestantism was born. But whether providential or not, it is a noteworthy fact that the discovery of America and the beginning of the Protestant Reformation, coming as they did within twenty-five years of one another, taken together, have large significance in the history of the colonization of the great continent of North America. The divisions and controversies created in western Europe as a consequence of the religious upheavals of the sixteenth and seventeenth centuries, furnished not only a large proportion of the principal leadership in the establishment of England's colonies in America, but also a considerable proportion of the colonists as well.

I

As is now well understood, there emerged out of the Reformation two distinct types of Protestantism, which have come to be characterized as right-wing and left-wing. Under the right-wing classification are included those Protestant Churches which were established by law in all the lands in western Europe where Protestantism gained the upper hand. On the continent Lutheran and Reformed Churches were established as the State religion in all the Protestant German states; in the Protestant cantons of Switzerland; in the Scandinavian countries, Denmark, Norway, and Sweden, and in Holland. In the British Isles the Presbyterian Church was by law established in Scotland and the Church of England became the only legal religion in England. These right-wing Churches were also confessional Churches, that is they

formulated elaborate creeds or confessions of faith which incorporated much of the theology that had developed throughout
the Christian centuries, only discarding the elaborate penitential
system which had developed in the later medieval Church. In
other words the right-wing Churches did not break entirely with
the past. As is well known the Church of England was completely
Catholic in both doctrine and worship until the adoption of the
Prayer Books in the reign of Edward the Sixth, and there are
many to-day within the Anglican Church, as well as in the Protestant Episcopal Church in the United States, who hold that their
Church has never been Protestant. In many respects the Church
of England was the most right-wing of all the revolting Churches.
Thus it came about that the right-wing phase of the Reformation
triumphed throughout western Europe and in the British Isles.

As a consequence of their important official status and of the
historic prominence of their principal leaders, such as Luther,
Calvin, Zwingli, and Cranmer, most well-informed people think
of the Reformation almost exclusively in terms of these right-wing
Churches. Such well-known histories of the Reformation as
Thomas M. Lindsay's[a] almost, if not quite completely, overlook
its left-wing phase. He devotes more than twenty chapters to the
several right-wing phases but only one brief chapter to the
Anabaptists or the left-wing beginnings. This is typical of other
treatments, at least until very recent times.

The left-wing type of Protestantism, as the name implies, was
radical, and, coming as it did out of the mass of the common
people, its leaders were of secondary importance, and therefore
were little known. In contrast to the right-wing Protestantism
these left-wing movements rejected all union between Church and
State and repudiated the right of the civil arm to interfere in any
way with matters of religion and conscience. In other words they
threw overboard all the developments in Church-State relationships which had taken place since the Council of Nicea. They also
differed from the right-wing phase of Protestantism in that they
stressed the inner, personal character of religion, played down its
institutional character, and put much less stress upon creeds and
sacraments. As Professor Batten states, 'this brand of Protestantism developed out of the spiritual strivings of the common man',[b]

[a] *A History of the Reformation*, 2 vols. (New York 1910).
[b] Joseph Minton Batten, 'The Independent Tradition', in *Protestantism: A Symposium*,
W. K. Anderson, ed., pp. 88–98 (Nashville 1944).

and was bound to become increasingly important in any society where the rights and privileges of the common man received recognition. A Roman Catholic historian has stated that the radical sects in the long run were to prove more characteristic of Protestantism than Luther or Calvin, because in their total impact they substitute 'individualistic for collective Christianity'.*a* All the great concepts for which American democracy stands to-day, individual rights, freedom of conscience, freedom of speech, self-government and complete religious liberty, are concepts coming out of the left-wing phase of the Reformation.*b*

In seventeenth-century Europe, left-wing Protestantism was everywhere under a legal ban; in the New World, on the other hand, it was to find a political and social soil suitable for its growth and development, and there it was that it came to full fruition.

II

As was to be expected, right-wing Protestantism was the first to be transplanted to the American colonies. Indeed, until about 1680 this type of Protestantism dominated the American colonial religious scene, resulting in the establishment by law of the Anglican Church in all the southern colonies, and partially in New York, where also the Church of Holland occupied an equally privileged position. The Congregationalists, the Church of the Puritans, though left-wing in the mother-country, soon developed distinctly right-wing attitudes in New England. It was established by law in the three New England colonies and became a confessional body when the Westminster Confession was incorporated in their first book of discipline (*The Cambridge Platform*, 1648). This led to the development of a persecuting complex and other attitudes entirely out of harmony with left-wing Protestantism.*c* By 1660 the European tradition of close Church-State relationship had been incorporated in all the colonies established up to that time except in Maryland and Rhode Island, both of

---

a Carlton J. H. Hayes, 'Significance of the Reformation in the Light of Contemporary Scholarship', *Catholic Hist. Review*, Vol. XVII, p. 157 (1932).

b For recent discussions of the left-wing phase of the Reformation see Ernest Sutherland Bates, *The American Faith: Its Religious, Political, and Economic Foundations* (New York 1940), especially Chapters 2 and 3. Also Roland H. Bainton, 'The Left Wing of the Reformation', *The Journal of Religion*, Vol. XXI, pp. 124–34 (April 1941).

c The long-continued persecution of Baptists and other protesting groups in New England brought numerous letters of protest from English Congregationalists; see particularly the letter of Robert Mascall, an English Congregationalist (25th March, 1669); W. W. Sweet, *Religion in Colonial America*, pp. 136–37 (New York 1942).

which had been founded by liberal-minded men, and under most unusual circumstances.

After 1690, however, a whole new set of liberalizing influences began to operate, which by the end of the colonial period had completely changed the entire colonial religious outlook. From this time forward right-wing Protestantism became increasingly less dominant, while left-wing attitudes spread widely throughout the colonies, particularly outside New England.

Four factors largely account for the triumph of left-wing Protestantism in eighteenth-century colonial America. The first was the kind and extent of the new immigration that began to flow to the colonies after 1690; a second was the influence exerted by the colonial revivals, which swept like a tidal wave throughout the colonies, beginning about 1725 and continuing intermittently until the opening of the war for Independence; a third was the effect of pioneering upon attitudes and ways of thinking; and a fourth the influence exerted by the wide acceptance of the natural rights philosophy by many Americans in the Revolutionary generation, and especially among the principal leaders, both political and religious.

1. English immigration to the colonies had largely ceased by 1660, though the Quaker colonies established after that date attracted many English Quakers. In the year 1690 the total population of the colonies numbered about 250,000, which was predominantly of English stock. By 1775 the population had increased to ten times that number and was approximately 2,500,000. This astonishing increase was largely due to a new non-English immigration, which began as a mere trickle in the 1680's with the coming of the Huguenots and by 1720 had become a German and Scotch-Irish flood. After 1690, population doubled every twenty-five years and by 1760 one-third of the population was foreign born.[a]

Beginning about 1697 German immigrants from the Rhineland, particularly, began to come to Pennsylvania, and the adjoining colonies of New York and Maryland. The Germans in the Rhine provinces had been the innocent victims of the ambition of Louis the Fourteenth to annex the Rhineland to his empire and between 1674 and 1704 a series of invasions devastated that whole area. Fields were laid waste, vineyards cut down, and

[a] Carl Wittke, *We who Built America* (New York 1940), especially Chapters 5 and 6. See also Arthur H. Hirsch, *The Huguenots of Colonial South Carolina* (Chapel Hill 1928).

thousands of people were driven from their homes. The situation was aggravated by crop failures and famine. Many died of exposure and starvation, and thousands found refuge in Switzerland and Holland. The sufferings of the Palatinate Germans aroused widespread sympathy in England which led Queen Anne to extend an invitation for them to seek a home in America. In the year 1690 some 30,000 were encamped near London seeking transportation to the colonies. Soon immigration to America became a mighty stream and threatened to depopulate the Rhine valley. Eventually some 150,000 to 200,000 Germans of various religious complexions found their way to the colonies, to them a land of hope.

The first Germans to come were the Mennonites and Dunkers and other left-wing groups as the Schwenkfelders, Moravians, but eventually the Reformed and Lutheran immigration greatly exceeded that of the sectaries. But the principal leadership among both the Lutheran and Reformed colonial Germans was pietistic, placing the principal emphasis upon inner, personal religion. Their leaders, such as Henry M. Muhlenberg, remained in close touch with the pietistic centres in Europe, such as Halle and Herrnhut. Since in their new environment there was no chance of their occupying a privileged position, they took on, more or less as a matter of course, the independent point of view, though retaining their historic confessions. Thus the total impact of the colonial Germans was that of independents.

The largest single racial group to find its way to colonial America, and the last to come, were the Scotch-Irish.[a] By the 1720's they were arriving in successive waves, which soon cut the population of Ulster in half. As many as 200,000 had arrived by the opening of the Revolution. They were the most widely distributed throughout the colonies of any immigration group, and there were at least five hundred distinct Scotch-Irish communities scattered throughout the thirteen colonies, from Maine on the north to Georgia on the South. Just as their forefathers had carried the Presbyterian system of polity and doctrine from Scotland to North Ireland, so the Scotch-Irish with equal tenacity brought their cultural and religious patterns to the New World. Though the Presbyterian Church was a State establishment in

[a] For a recent summary of the several causes for the Scotch-Irish immigration see W. W. Sweet, *Religion in Colonial America*, pp. 245–54; also Wayland F. Dunaway, *The Scotch-Irish of Colonial Pennsylvania* (Chapel Hill 1944), especially Chapter 2, 'The Ulster Background of the Scotch-Irish'.

Scotland, it was a dissenting body in North Ireland. There they were under the hated domination of the Established Church of Ireland, for the support of which they were compelled to pay tithes. Their ministers were disqualified from performing marriages, while the Test Act of 1704 excluded them from all military and civil office. The Bench of Bishops in the Irish House of Lords were the principal instigators of these civil and religious disabilities, and as a consequence the Scotch-Irish brought with them to the New World a burning hatred of Church establishments and bishops. Froude tells us that 'the resentment which they carried with them continued to burn in their new homes; and in the War for Independence England had no fiercer enemies than the grandsons and great-grandsons of the Presbyterians who had held Ulster against Tyrconnell', nor were there any Tories or pacifists in their ranks.

> And when the day of trial came
> Of which we know the story,
> No Erin son of Scottish blood
> Was ever found a Tory.

An influence which helped to speed up eighteenth-century immigration to the colonies was the fact that all the colonies established after 1660 were proprietary grants. That is, they were all great land ventures, not trading enterprises, depending for their success upon attracting as many colonists as possible to take up land. As a consequence, the proprietors of these new colonies in process of formation vied with one another in making their colonies as attractive as possible to prospective colonists. Among other inducements they threw down all religious barriers, hoping thereby to attract the dissenting elements in Protestant Europe. Penn, in his promotion literature for his great province of Pennsylvania, laid particular stress upon the freedom of religion, as did also the proprietors of the Carolinas and Georgia.[a]

2. There is a close relationship between this great eighteenth-century immigration and the rise of the colonial revivals. It was this tremendous influx of European people; the consequent settlement of new regions; and the pushing of pioneers into the back country that called for new methods and new emphasis in organized religion. The old ways would no longer suffice if

[a] Reba C. Strickland, *Religion and the State in Georgia in the Eighteenth Century* (New York 1940). For the many religious groups among the Georgia settlers see pp. 35–43.

religion was to be brought to bear upon the swarming new population. Freedom from family ties, church connexions, and the influences and restraints of the community life of the Old World were an invitation to indulgences and loose ways of living in the New, which would have been shunned in the old home surroundings. Consequently, by the end of the first third of the eighteenth century there were more unchurched people in the colonies in proportion to the population than was to be found anywhere in Christendom.

This relatively small number of Church members in eighteenth-century colonial America was not only due to the scattered nature of the population and the rough and rude conditions which inevitably accompany pioneering, but also because of certain barriers the Churches themselves erected, and the voluntary nature of Church membership which did not come about as a matter of course, but in every case it was a matter of personal decision. The Congregationalists and Baptists required the relation of a satisfactory religious experience before the congregation for full communion, while the absence of an Anglican bishop made Confirmation impossible in colonial America. Thus the Anglican Church was made up of unconfirmed people, which would mean that only the most earnest would consider themselves communicants.[a]

By the end of the seventeenth century the colonial religious leaders were becoming painfully aware of the decline of religion and morality among the colonists, and this awareness was a deciding factor in starting the great awakenings, which swept throughout the colonies during the middle years of the eighteenth century.[b]

It will not be necessary to follow the course of the revivals in detail. They were not an extension of the evangelical movement in England, as has often been stated. Nor was Jonathan Edwards the father of revivalism in America. The American revivals began twelve years before John Wesley's heart-warming experience, while the Middle colony revival ante-dated the Edwardian revival in New England by eight years. Rather, the revivals arose out of a situation that was universal throughout the colonies. As in England, the revivals were rooted in pietism and not in Calvinism, although all the great colonial revivalists were Calvinists, until

[a] See the questionnaire sent out to all Anglican parishes in America by the Bishop of London in 1724.

[b] W. W. Sweet, *Revivalism in America: Its Origin, Growth, and Decline* (New York 1944). See particularly Chapter 1, 'Setting the Stage'.

B

Methodism was introduced in the final phase—but it was a Calvinism impregnated with pietism which rendered it effective in reaching the hearts of individuals.

The doctrine stressed by all the revivalists, and especially those of the middle and southern colonies, was the equality of all men in the sight of God. They sought to reach all classes; rich as well as poor; masters as well as slaves; the ignorant as well as the educated. In spite of the prevailing Calvinism of colonial Protestantism, the revivalists made no distinction in their appeals, with the result that the revivals were a great levelling influence in American colonial society and sowed broadcast the seeds of democracy. The revivals transcended denominational lines and theological differences. In a sense they marked the beginning of what might be termed the peculiar American emphasis in Christianity in that the chief stress was placed upon results and not formal creeds, upon correct living rather than upon a correct doctrine. Complicated theologies were reduced to a few simple points and principles which the common man could comprehend, and the emphasis was upon the personal rather than the institutional.[a] The needs of the Church as such were subordinated to the needs of men. George Whitefield, who spent more than ten years of his life in his American ministry, covered the entire inhabited parts of America in his many preaching tours. He identified himself with no single religious body, but served them all without favouritism. Though an Anglican priest, his work in America was almost completely outside his own communion. In fact, the colonial Anglicans profited less from the awakenings than any other religious body.[b]

Previous to the great Awakenings organized religion in the Colonies was largely an upper-class affair, and a matter of the few. Of the two State Churches established by law in nine of the thirteen colonies was this particularly true. Although the New England Awakening revived and strengthened Congregationalism, it also brought on controversy and division. The net result of colonial revivalism was greatly to increase the number of

---

[a] W. M. Gewehr, *The Great Awakening in Virginia* (Chapel Hill 1930). See particularly Chapter 8, 'Contributions to the Rise of Democracy'. The undenominational character of Whitefield's American ministry is emphasized in Charles H. Maxson, *The Great Awakening in the Middle Colonies* (Chicago 1920), Chapter 8, 'Whitefield the Pacificator'.

[b] For recent summaries of the Colonial Awakenings see W. W. Sweet, *Religion in Colonial America*, Chapter 9, 'Religion reaches the Masses: the Great Awakenings'; and W. W. Sweet, *Revivalism in America*, etc., Chapters 2–6.

dissenters, and by the end of the colonial period they were in the majority in all the colonies outside New England.

3. A third influence which tended to strengthen left-wing ideas during the colonial period was the total effect of pioneering upon ideas and attitudes. The pioneer must of necessity develop a high degree of self-dependence if he is to survive. He becomes a self-reliant individualist, inclined to go his own way with little regard for the traditional ways of doing things. He believed in complete social equality. In many instances a major motive in his migration from the Old World to the New was to escape the social inequalities and depressing conventions of the older communities. 'Equal distribution of property', as Albert Gallatin stated, 'made every individual independent and produced a true and real equality.'

In Edmund Burke's well-known speech in Parliament on 'Conciliation with America', delivered on 22nd March 1775, occurs this remarkably accurate summary of the religious situation in America on the eve of the American Revolution. He states that one of the reasons for resistance to England on the part of the colonists was their individualistic manner of expressing their religion. Their religion was the most extreme Protestantism of the Protestant religion. Their beliefs had advanced beyond all others 'in the liberty of the Reformation'. Existing in a large variety of denominations, they agree in nothing but in the communion of the spirit of liberty. When the colonists left England, the spirit of dissent was high in the Mother country, and among the immigrants it was the highest of all. Of the stream of foreigners which had constantly flowed into the colonies, the greatest part was composed of dissenters from the establishments in the several countries from which they had come, and they therefore brought with them a temper and character in harmony with the people with whom they mingled. The colonists had accustomed themselves to the freest debate on all religious subjects, and so far had individualism developed in religion that even women were permitted to have opinions and it was said that 'every man's hat was his Church'.[a] Thus the natural inclination of the pioneer would be left-wing in his religious ideas, and since the great majority were out of touch with the Church, or only remotely in touch with organized religion, they were thus forced to be self-dependent in their religious life.

[a] E. F. Humphrey, *Nationalism and Religion in America* (Boston 1924), pp. 20–2.

4. While the common man in eighteenth-century colonial America was becoming increasingly left-wing in his religious views, as a result of the new immigration, the revivals, and pioneering, many of the leaders of American colonial society were reaching the same position through quite a different set of influences. The writings of John Locke, who became the American philosopher *par excellence* in the eighteenth century was one of these influences. In his *Two Treatises of Government* (1690), *The Reasonableness of Christianity as Delivered in the Scriptures*, which appeared in 1695, and especially in his four *Letters on Toleration* (1689–1706), all of which had great vogue in eighteenth-century America, Locke, convincingly and with clarity, argues for the separation of Church and State. He insisted that the Church is a society completely voluntary and free; that it results from men joining themselves together of their own accord, for the worshipping of God. Though he considered himself a good Anglican, he repudiated the notion that a true Church was dependent upon its having bishops and presbyters whose authority was delivered from the Apostles and continued down to the present time by an uninterrupted succession. He contended that no religious body had a monopoly of orthodoxy, since there is no authority on earth that can judge between Churches about the truth of their doctrines. In any controversy therefore between Churches over such matters 'both sides are equal', because all men are free from all dominion over one another in matters of religion.

Locke agreed completely with the left-wing Protestants in holding that religion was primarily a personal concern. No man can be saved, he argued, by a religion he distrusts or by a worship which he abhors. Like Roger Williams, Locke contended that Christ instituted no commonwealth, prescribed for His followers no new or peculiar form of government, nor did He put the sword in any magistrate's hand with the commission to use it in forcing any man to forsake his own religion and receive His. Liberty of conscience is every man's right, and there should be no compulsion in matters of religion. Indeed, in 1681 Locke was led to write a defence of the left-wing position, entitled *A Defence of Non-Conformity*, in reply to two treatises which had been published by Edward Stillingfleet, then Dean of St. Paul's, against dissenters. Locke was greatly influenced by dissenter points of view,[a] and he

---

[a] H. R. Fox Bourne, *The Life of John Locke* (2 vols.). Vol. I, pp. 456–60 (New York 1876). See also J. M. Mecklin, *The Story of American Dissent*, pp. 342–8 (New York 1934). Locke's *Defence of Non-Conformity* was never published.

in turn passed them on to the American leaders in the Revolutionary generation, such as Madison and Jefferson. Thus it came about that not only had the great majority of the people become imbued with the left-wing Protestant position on the freedom of conscience and the separation of Church and State, but many of the leaders in the rising new nation had come to accept the same point of view.[a]

It was the triumph of left-wing Protestantism in eighteenth-century colonial America which underlay the final achievement of the separation of Church and State. When American colonization began there was not a nation in Christendom that did not have an established Church, and it was universally believed that the maintenance of a uniform religion in a nation was essential for the safety and unity of the State. This was true both in Protestant as well as in Catholic countries. Even in nine of the thirteen colonies, there were Church establishments, although only in Congregational New England and in Anglican Virginia did the legal religion represent a majority. With the coming of independence the general state of mind throughout the new nation was such that religious freedom and the separation of Church and State were inevitable. Only in Virginia and New England was there a serious attempt to retain Church establishments, and even there complete separation was not long delayed. The embodiment of the great principles of religious freedom in the new State constitutions, and finally in the Federal constitution, was simply translating an overwhelming public opinion and colonial experience into the fundamental law of the land.

The most left-wing of all the major present-day American religious bodies are the Baptists, whose first great principle, the complete separation of Church and State, may truly be called the Magna Charta of all our liberties. Today all American Protestantism accepts that principle. Even American Roman Catholicism renders it lip service, though they repudiate it in principle.

Not only did the triumph of left-wing Protestantism constitute one of the principal factors in the achievement of our basic freedoms, it also was responsible for developing attitudes and emphases in religion which, at least, help to account for American activism. Those Protestant countries in western Europe in which the Church has been tied most closely to the State have been

[a] For a much fuller discussion of this statement see W. W. Sweet, 'Natural Religion and Religious Liberty' (The Dudleian Lecture at Harvard University 1944), *Harvard Divinity School Bulletin*, 1944–5.

those areas in which quietism has principally flourished. Indeed, it is not far wrong to say that quietism and confessionalism are characteristics of State Churches. In countries where such matters as social and economic justice, public morals, and education are State concerns, the Church occupies a strictly circumscribed and limited place in the life of the people. Thus the principal concern of the State Church and clergy is confined to purely religious matters, such as public worship and the maintenance of the official theology. On the other hand, in such countries as the United States, where the law does not attempt to define the specific functions of the Church, or the exact part religion is to play in the life of the nation, the Church will be more inclined to attempt to permeate all of life. Thus the concept of the part that the Church is to play in society is greatly widened since it conceives of its task, not simply that of maintaining worship, but also that of righting wrongs through influences exerted upon the public conscience, either by direct or indirect means.

As Troeltsch has correctly stated, the separation of Church and State in America is a political, not a social, separation. Though Christianity is not the State religion, its influence permeates the nation and the United States upholds and defends what we call Christian civilization. While any direct participation of the Church in politics would be universally condemned yet it is generally considered that religious influences are needed to undergird our social and political life, and that in matters of moral concern it is the Church's duty to influence public opinion.[a]

[a] W. A. Visser t' Hooft, *The Background of the Social Gospel in America* (Haarlem 1928), pp. 19–20.

CHAPTER TWO

RELIGION IN THE WINNING OF THE WEST[a]

FROM THE beginning of colonization to more or less recent times America has always had somewhere a frontier; a new, raw, undeveloped region into which a restless population was rapidly moving and in which new communities were as rapidly forming. Every section of the country, from the Atlantic seaboard to the Pacific slope, at one time or another, passed through this frontier stage. Each of these successive frontier regions developed similar characteristics. In all of them the economic urge was dominant, at least during the early stages of development. Generally speaking, the pioneers in each of the frontiers were young people, looking for better economic opportunities. They were full of courage, impatient of restraint, lovers of liberty and firm believers in the doctrine of equality. They were absorbed in the building of a society more democratic than that which was to be found anywhere else in the world. Away from the restraints of an older established society, innovations were readily introduced and as readily accepted. They were not afraid to entertain new ideas or to modify or throw overboard old ones which they found ill-adapted to the new conditions which they faced. They were not only engaged in the exhilarating task of building a new earth in which there was to be greater opportunities for themselves and their children, but their leaders, at least, visualized also a new heaven.

In the task of building this new society in the west the religious forces played a large and essential part. In this uncouth and raw frontier society there was much irreligion and scoffing at the things of the Spirit. The woods were full of blatant professed infidels, some of whom vowed that the Christian Sabbath should never be established in the west. But this was by no means true of all, or even a majority. A people inspired 'by the sense of a career of future greatness can seldom fail to develop active religious life in some form', and it was certain that the American

[a] W. W. Sweet, *Religion on the American Frontier*: Vol. I, *The Baptists* (New York 1931); Vol. II, *The Presbyterians* (Chicago 1936); Vol. III, *The Congregationalists* (Chicago 1939); Vol. IV, *The Methodists* (Chicago 1946).

frontiersman would eventually become interested in religion and education. Indeed, there were to be found on every American frontier from the beginning some who realized that man cannot live by bread alone.

For the first two generations following independence the most outstanding fact in the history of the United States was the westward movement of population; the building of new communities; the forming of new territories; the admission of new States into the Union. From 1791 to 1821 eleven new States were added to the original thirteen—and the most important work performed by the American Churches during this formative period was that of following this restless and moving population with the refining and uplifting influences of religion. The first danger which always accompanies any great migration of people, as Horace Bushnell so well pointed out more than a hundred years ago, is that of reverting to barbarism. Cut off from the restraints and refining influences of the old home and of the old home communities, with their churches and schools and family relationships, and living under rude and uncouth conditions, many a frontier family lost track of the Sabbath and gave up all attempts at refinement and decency in living. Many frontier communities became notorious for lawlessness, rowdyism, gambling, swearing, drinking, and fighting. Travellers in the trans-Allegheny west in the early part of the last century were often 'terrified at the drunkenness, the vice, the gambling, the brutal fights, the gouging, the needless duels they beheld on every hand'.[a] Their social gatherings, such as log-rollings, house-raisings, and even weddings and funerals often degenerated into drunken orgies, where

> *There was lots of swearing,*
> *Of boasting and daring,*
> *Of fighting and tearing.*

For at least fifty years following independence a vast struggle was going on between the Alleghenies and the Mississippi River; between civilization and Christian morality on the one hand, and barbarism on the other, and upon the outcome of that struggle hung the fate of the new nation.

Let us glance for a moment at the religious forces which were available to meet this crisis.

[a] For the moral disintegration found on the early frontier see W. W. Sweet, 'The Churches as Moral Courts of the Frontier', *Church History*, Vol. II, No. 1, March 1933).

At the head of the list were the Congregationalists, the largest and most influential religious body at the end of the colonial period. Established by law in Massachusetts, Connecticut, and New Hampshire, Congregationalism possessed about seven hundred congregations and had a native and American trained ministry. Next in point of size were the Presbyterians with some six hundred congregations, and they too possessed a well-educated ministry, mostly American trained. Ranking third in point of size were the Baptists, ministering primarily to humble and un-churched people, but growing rapidly as a result of that fact and their development of a devoted farmer-preacher type of ministry. Fourth on the list were the Episcopalians, though at the moment under a cloud of suspicion due to the unpopularity which the struggle for independence had brought upon them. There were also some two hundred and ninety-five Quaker meetings; two hundred and fifty Dutch and German Reformed congregations; some two hundred Lutheran congregations; perhaps some fifty or sixty congregations of German sectaries; a bare fifty Roman Catholic; and thirty-seven Methodist circuits, then nominally still a part of the Anglican Communion. Such were the forces of organized religion in the new nation upon which the respon-sibility was largely placed of saving America for Christian civilization.

It was the way in which the task of following the population westward was faced by these several religious bodies that was to determine which of the Churches were to become large and which were to remain small; which were to be sectional and which were to be national. It was perhaps unfortunate that the two most privileged religious bodies of the colonial period, the Con-gregationalists and the Episcopalians, failed to take advantage of the opportunities and responsibilities that the great westward movement presented. Neither of them at the beginning took a national view of their task. Both also were handicapped by an unfortunate superiority complex, which came naturally from the fact that both had been State Churches and possessed privileges and social status which in the long run was to prove a handicap rather than an advantage to their growth and influence. Their appeal was, to a large degree, limited to the more prosperous groups, and they became, in a sense, apostles only to the genteel.

Others of the colonial religious bodies faced other handicaps. The Dutch, the German Reformed, and the Lutherans, together with the German sectaries were still foreign-language bodies, and thus their activity and their appeal was limited to a particular class of people. As a consequence, they did not possess a national view of their task and they were destined to continue to minister only to small sections of the population—to people of their own language and cultural background. The Presbyterians were also handicapped in something of the same way. Their ministers on frontier preaching tours sought out communities where people of Scotch or Scotch-Irish background were to be found, and were not greatly concerned with communities in which there were no people of their own kind. To a large degree also the Congregational home missionaries were inclined to seek out communities of New England settlers, and made little effort to reach a cross section of frontier society. The Quakers after their adoption of the birth-right membership in 1734 soon lost their burning missionary zeal and settled down to become a smug, self-satisfied, and economically prosperous social group.

Thus it was that the great task of following population west, by a sort of process of elimination, came to be more and more the responsibility of the Churches of the poor—principally the Baptists and Methodists and, to a limited degree, the Presbyterians. These three American Churches made the greatest moral and religious impact upon the first two generations of the American frontier. Each had its own method of performing its frontier task. The Baptist farmer-preacher came along with the people pushing westward. He was sent by no Church organization, and though with little or no formal education he preached the Gospel to his neighbours as he understood it, and what he lacked in education he partly made up in earnestness and devotion. The Presbyterian minister in the early west was at least half a schoolteacher. Since he was generally a man of education, the popular sentiment of the community where he resided compelled him to open a school. The Baptist preacher must make his own living and thus he divided his energies between his farm and his church, his plough and his pulpit; the Presbyterian schoolteacher-preacher divided his time between his schoolteaching and his preaching; the Methodist circuit rider, on the other hand, gave all his time to his religious activities. On great circuits, sometimes as large as three or four hundred miles around, he preached at least once every day in the week, with the possible exception of Monday, and during the course of a single year travelled many thousands of miles. So closely did the Methodist system enable the circuit preacher to follow the moving population that not infrequently a circuit rider would call at a settler's cabin before the mud in the stick chimney was dry, or before the weight poles were on the roof. Methodism was so organized as to be able to follow step by step this moving population, and to carry the Gospel even to the most distant cabin. It alone could be present whenever a grave was opened, or an infant was found in its cradle.

The relative effectiveness of these most important religious bodies may be visualized by some statistics. In the census of 1820 there were some 21,000 Methodists in Kentucky; over 20,000 Baptists; the Presbyterians had 3,700 members; while all other bodies numbered not more than 500; and this proportion pretty generally prevailed throughout the trans-Allegheny region. By 1850 the Methodists had become the largest Protestant body in America, with a membership of 1,324,000; the Baptists numbered 815,000; the Presbyterians came third with 487,000; the Congregationalists fourth with 197,000; the Lutherans had 163,000; the Disciples 118,000; and the Episcopalians 90,000.

There were reasons, however, other than that the Methodists had the most effective ecclesiastical machinery for following the population westward, which must be noted if we are to understand the phenomenal growth of John Wesley's disciples in the west.

The rapid expansion of early American Methodism cannot be explained apart from Francis Asbury, the universally respected leader throughout these formative years. Coming to America in 1771, one of the eight official representatives of the English Conference to be sent to America previous to the Revolution, he was the only one to remain and become a full-fledged American citizen. His first great contribution was to revive the circuit system, which had been largely shunted aside by his predecessors, and to shape it to meet American needs. He was the principal link between John Wesley and the American Methodists during the crisis years of the Revolutionary war. Indeed, without his wise guidance that link might well have been severed, due to Wesley's sweeping condemnation of the American rebels. During these years something was taking place in the American mind which the aged Wesley was incapable of understanding and it was Asbury who bridged the widening breach, and made it possible for the father of Methodism to retain his spiritual leadership among the American Methodists, even though they were no longer willing to receive his every word as law.

The quiet assurance with which Asbury assumed leadership at the organizing Conference in 1784, even in the face of Wesley's instructions giving precedence to Dr. Thomas Coke, was soon recognized by Coke himself as necessary. Asbury was fully aware that the American Methodists would never accept the dictum of an Englishman, especially during the years immediately following independence. It is a revealing fact that Dr. Coke, even though his presence in America was appreciated by both the preachers and people, was never permitted to preside independently at any Conference in America, nor did he ever assign the preachers to their circuits.

The formation of the Methodist Episcopal Church in 1784 as an independent ecclesiastical body, gave Asbury's genius for leadership an ever-widening scope, while his example of courageous and selfless devotion to the spreading of scriptural holiness throughout the land was a major factor in raising up an ever-increasing number of devoted preachers willing and anxious to follow in his train. The power he wielded over the far-flung and ever-expanding American Methodism for more than thirty years can only be explained in the light of his saintly character and organizing genius, two qualities which he shared with his spiritual father, John Wesley. Indeed, what Wesley was to England, Asbury was to America. Both were prophets of the long road. Certain it is there was no other American religious leadership in the early years of the new nation's life which was so conspicuous for its adequacy in meeting the major needs of a society in motion as was that of Francis Asbury.[a]

The Methodists of those days were possessed of a burning zeal for the advancement of the kingdom of God. As was said of the early Quakers, so it could be said of them, the Gospel was as a hammer and an anvil in them. It drove them forth into every nook and corner of the needy land, and they considered the vast continent as their parish. Although the smallest and most humble of American religious bodies at the opening of the national period,

[a] For recent appraisals of Francis Asbury's place in the history of American Methodism see W. W. Sweet, *Methodism in American History* (New York 1933). The most recent biographies of Asbury are E. S. Tipple, *Francis Asbury: The Prophet of the Long Road* (New York 1916), and James Lewis, *Francis Asbury: Bishop of the Methodist Episcopal Church* (London 1927).

the Methodists were the first to achieve a national organization, suited to an indefinite geographic expansion.

Another reason which helps explain Methodism's success was its catholicity. It built no ecclesiastical or theological fences to keep men out.

There is no such thing as a distinctive Methodist theology. Those Churches which possess the historical confessions have been contemptuous of Methodism in the past, and many of them still are, because of this fact. This does not mean, however, that Methodists have not been interested in theology or considered it of slight importance. Methodists have in fact produced some very respectable theologians on both sides of the Atlantic. There was no other religious body in seventeenth-century England that gave more attention to the discussion of theology than did Wesley's Conferences. But he was always careful to preface these discussions with the statement: 'You must not expect me to come to your opinion, nor will I expect you to come to mine. We can no more think alike than we can see or hear alike.' But he always concluded, 'We can all love alike'. There was but one condition of membership to Methodist societies—the desire to flee from the wrath to come. Wesley took pride in the fact that no doctrinal tests were ever laid down. On many occasions he stated: 'Methodists do not impose, in order to their admission, any opinions whatever. Let them hold particular or general redemption, absolute or conditional decrees; let them be churchmen, or dissenters, Presbyterians or Independents, it is no obstacle. Let them choose one mode of baptism or another, it is no bar to their admission. The Presbyterian may be a Presbyterian still; the Independent and Anabaptist use his own worship still. So may the Quaker; and none will contend with him about it. They think and let think. One condition, and only one, is required —a real desire to save the soul. Where this is, it is enough; they desire no more; they lay stress upon nothing else; they only ask, "Is thy heart herein as my heart? If it be, give me thy hand".'

None of the divisions that have occurred in American Methodism have been due to differences in theology; and one of the principal reasons why the Methodists, alone of the three great Churches which divided over the slavery issue, have been able to heal that greatest of all schisms in American Protestantism is largely due to that fact. There were no basic theological differences between the three Methodist bodies which came together in 1939 to form the present Methodist Church.

As a consequence of this attitude toward theology, Methodism, with one or two regrettable exceptions, has been free from heresy trials. For Methodism possesses no theological measuring rod to determine when one is a heretic. It has plenty of machinery to try a heretic if one could be found, but has no way to determine when one is found. Contrast this with the Presbyterians. They possess not only the machinery to try heretics, but also one of the most effective theological measuring rods ever devised, in the Westminster Confession. It is not surprising, therefore, that they have produced the most numerous as well as the most famous heresy trials in American ecclesiastical annals. In the 1850's in the little town of Princeton, Illinois, there were eleven kinds of Presbyterians at one time, and at about the same time in Bloomington, Indiana, there were eight varieties.

Pretty generally, the great evangelical Churches in America have gone forward on the assumption that man and God must work together to build a decent world; that no situation could be so bad but that man with God's help could do something about it. In the face of frontier hardships and dangers, surrounded by crude and raw conditions of life, which of necessity must always accompany pioneering, the western pioneers, like the New England Puritans, succeeded in maintaining a cosmic optimism even in the midst of anguish. They were too busy waging war against sin, too intoxicated with the exultation of the never-ending conflict, to find occasional reverses, however costly, a cause for deep and permanent discouragement.

One of the principal characteristics of America from the beginning, and particularly during the period of the settlement of the trans-Allegheny regions and the great prairie-plains beyond, has been an immense optimism. Opportunity has been a charmed word throughout our history. It is not incorrect to say that the greatest accomplishment of the American people has been the conquest of the continent. Not only has the mere filling in of vast unoccupied areas with a teeming population been a notable achievement, but far more notable has been the establishment throughout the nation of American democratic, political, and social institutions; and if the story of American industrial achievements is a fascinating romance it is not more so than is that of the story of the founding and development of American educational and cultural institutions. Naturally, out of such a background have come optimistic and positive attitudes toward life; the attitude that no obstacle is too great to be overcome in any realm.

Here certainly is one of the roots of the American emphasis upon social Christianity; the influences which have come directly out of frontier experiences. It is significant that those Churches that have been the strongest supporters and promoters of the Social Gospel are those which came to power and influence as a consequence of their successful coping with the frontier—the Baptists, the Methodists, the Presbyterians, the Disciples, and the Congregationalists. It was in the pioneering period that they learned the necessity of making application of Christian principles to society. Frontier Baptist, Methodist, and Presbyterian Churches disciplined members not only for personal lapses, such as drunkenness and immorality, but also brought them to book for fraudulent business dealings—such as selling unsound horses, removing boundary stones, or cutting down corner trees. Frontier preachers as a matter of course took part in politics, and it was perfectly normal and natural that the first Governor of Ohio, Edward Tiffin, should have been a Methodist local preacher, and that one of the early Governors of Kentucky was a Baptist farmer-preacher. Peter Cartwright was a member of the Illinois legislature for two terms, and while there introduced the first measure for the establishment of a State college. He was in active politics for many years; he was high in the councils of the Jacksonian party and in 1846 was their candidate for Congress, running against Abraham Lincoln. Thus religion tended to permeate all frontier society—and when new frontiers arose, created by the new industrial developments and the rise of the great cities, the movement to bring religion to bear upon the new social problems thus created was not something new, but was simply the revival of a frontier emphasis, applied to a much more complicated and difficult social situation.

CHAPTER THREE

REVIVALISM IN AMERICAN PROTESTANTISM

REVIVALISM in American colonial Protestantism began as a way of meeting situations produced as a consequence of the great migrations of European peoples to the New World in the eighteenth century. It has persisted through several generations because, until recent times, conditions similar to those which produced it have continued to exist in many sections of the nation. In the process of the peopling of the North American continent the transplanting of society from older to newer sections was a long continuing process, lasting to within a generation of our own time. New frontiers were in constant process of formation, and people were continually moving westward. Thus American society through much of its history may be characterized as a society in motion, which meant that people were continually moving away from older communities and forming new ones. In such a society it takes time for institutions to take root, for such a society is always strongly individualistic. Revivalism arose in such a society as a way of bringing Christianity to individuals; and revivalism flourished in frontier society because it was religion applied to individual needs.

Revivalism stressed the fact that salvation depended upon personal decisions. Religion was an inner matter; not an institutional affair. It meant the personal acceptance of Christ as Saviour and not simply an intellectual assent to a credal statement.

There arose in the west two more or less distinctive types of revivalism.[a] One was the Presbyterian-Congregational or a Calvinistic revivalism. This has been termed 'rational' revivalism, in which there was 'no wildness and extravagance' and 'very little commotion of the animal feelings'. This type of revivalism insisted that the Gospel be preached in all its Calvinistic purity; that if it were to have any effect the people must be well instructed in the doctrines of Christianity, which meant, of course, that its appeal was meant only for those well grounded in the Shorter Catechism.

[a] For a discussion of the two types of revivalism in the American west see W. W. Sweet, *Revivalism in America: Its Origin, Growth, and Decline* (New York 1944), pp. 124–8.

But the great mass of the frontier population had neither been instructed in the Catechism nor in the truths of the Bible. Thus this type of revivalism made only a limited appeal and would necessarily leave the great majority of the people untouched. The second kind of revivalism was the Methodist-Baptist-Disciple type, whose primary work was to take Christianity to the great mass of the religiously illiterate. The first type offered salvation to the few; the second offered it to all. The former was aristocratic; the latter democratic.

A phase of frontier revivalism which has been widely publicized is the camp-meeting. It has been the victim of much cheap debunking on the part of those whose primary interest has been in the spectacular and the unusual. But as a matter of fact, the camp-meeting became a most important and useful institution at least for the first two generations of the last century. Begun by the Presbyterians on the frontiers of Kentucky and Tennessee, as a result of the drawing power of an extraordinary frontier Presbyterian preacher, James McGready, it soon spread throughout the newer sections of the country. The greatest number of people ever gathered together in a frontier camp-meeting was at Cane Ridge in Bourbon county, Kentucky, in August 1801. Although under Presbyterian management, it attracted people of all denominations, as well as literally thousands who had no religious affiliation, many of them roughs and rowdies. Here there were many awe-inspiring happenings. Great numbers fell to the ground in what was called the 'falling exercise'; others got the 'jerks', and there was constant noise and confusion. This meeting marked the turning point in the history of the camp-meeting. To those accustomed to dignity and quietness in worship such confusion was distasteful, and many considered it a travesty upon religion. From this time Presbyterians divided over revivalism and the camp-meeting, resulting in the emergence of the Cumberland Presbyterians, favouring their continuance; and from this time forward the camp-meeting became primarily a Methodist institution.

So rapidly did the number of camp-meetings multiply that by 1811 there were more than four hundred; and by 1820 there were something near a thousand. While the camp-meeting was of large significance as a harvest time for the Methodists particularly, it has been much over-emphasized. Many have assumed that it represented about all there was of religious influence and activity

C

in the west. Yet the camp-meeting was never recognized as an official Methodist institution. There was never any legislation in the conferences regarding it, nor official rules devised for its management, but was always considered as an extra occasion in the economy of Methodism.

There has been too much stress placed upon the emotional excesses of camp-meetings and all too little upon the routine work of the frontier Churches and preachers. All the more aggressive frontier Churches stressed the necessity of conversion, and all of them had their own way of helping to bring it about. But once the convert was made and admitted to the Church as a member, he was brought under a discipline almost unbelievably strict.[a] This was true of Baptists, Methodists, and Presbyterians particularly. Nor was their religion all emotion. Frontier religion is far more solidly based than is usually pictured. The long lists of books, Bibles, testaments, hymn-books, disciplines, and the large number of subscribers to the *Christian Advocate and Journal*, Barton W. Stone's *Christian Messenger*, and other religious periodicals in the early west is evidence of the religious instruction afforded. The fact that almost all the early Presbyterian ministers in the west were also schoolteachers is evidence that theirs was a teaching as well as a preaching ministry.[b]

With the rapid changes in the cultural, economic, social, and religious climate which took place in the United States following the Civil War, the revivalistic emphasis among the evangelical Churches rapidly declined. Education, refinement, and dignity now characterized the ministry of an increasing number of Methodists, Baptists, and Disciples, while the Methodists particularly went far beyond the Presbyterians and Congregationalists, instituting forms and ritual in their worship. The old camp-meeting grounds, many of them still owned by Camp-Meeting Associations, were being changed into middle-class summer resorts or meeting places for summer Conferences. One of the old Methodist camp-meeting grounds, that at Chautauqua, New York, was after 1874 rapidly transformed into an educational institution which influenced the entire nation and inaugurated the Chautauqua Movement, an attempt to bring education in homœopathic doses to the masses.

[a] See W. W. Sweet, *The Churches as Moral Courts of the Frontier*. Also W. W. Sweet, *Religion on the American Frontier*, 4 vols.

[b] See *Benjamin Lakin Papers* (MSS. in University of Chicago collection). These contain lists of books sold on his circuits from year to year.

The rapid growth of American cities after 1880, particularly due to the drawing power of manufacturing centres upon rural and small-town people, and to an even greater degree upon people from the overcrowded countries of western Europe, created a religious situation in the cities which brought into existence the last phase of revivalism.

The flocking of both native and foreign-born people to the cities created problems of all sorts not only affecting government and social conditions, but also religion. Tens of thousands of these new city-dwellers lost contact with the Churches, and it was in the attempt to create in them a renewed religious interest that the great city revivalistic campaigns were inaugurated, which flourished for a generation, beginning with Dwight L. Moody. It was the city which gave rise to the professional revivalist, not the least among whom was Gypsy Smith, the English Methodist evangelist. It is an interesting and significant fact that in the history of American revivalism by far the largest number of famous revivalists have been either Presbyterians or Congregationalists, beginning with Gilbert Tennent and Jonathan Edwards in the eighteenth century, and ending with William A. Sunday.

Outside the Southern Baptists the revivalistic techniques have largely disappeared among the large evangelical Churches. The waning of revivalism among these large bodies has been one of the principal reasons for the emergence of numerous revivalistic sects, most of them stressing holiness and premillennialism. Appealing largely to people of the lower economic and cultural level of American society, they flourished as never before during the period of the great depression and the First and Second World Wars. The very fact that they have increased so rapidly in the last several years would seem to indicate they are supplying needs in reaching people which, at the present time at least, seem beyond the power of the middle-class Churches either to reach or supply. Methodism, once a great religious ferment, largely among the poor, has now become an upper-middle-class Church. Once it was proud to be called the poor man's Church; now it boasts of its colleges and universities, its great endowments and tremendous corporate power. Much the same thing is true of the Northern Baptists and in a more limited degree of the Disciples. The Episcopalians, the Presbyterians, and the Congregationalists are still more 'upper-class'. This is a trend which is a cause of great concern among the leaders in American Protestantism. If the century ahead is to be the century of the common man, nothing can be more important for the future of Christianity in America than for the great evangelical Churches to find the ways by which the well-trained minister can function at all levels of society. The notion often held in America that the most effective way to reach poor and ignorant people is to have religion brought to them by ignorant preachers is as ridiculous as it would be to say that in order to raise the health level of the poor and the ignorant we must have ignorant physicians. Here is a problem which cries for solution in every one of the major Protestant Churches in America.[a]

Stressing primarily the moral life and giving little attention to theological interests, revivalism tended to over-emphasize the good of man as the final aim in human action and to encourage the belief in the perfectibility of man and society. As a consequence, revivalism resulted in numerous by-products, some of them good, others harmful if not decidedly bad. Colonial and early nineteenth-century revivalism was directly or indirectly responsible for the great college movement. At least five of the nine colonial colleges sprang directly out of the colonial revivals, and an overwhelming proportion of the colleges established from independence to the Civil War had some direct relationship to revivalism. The listing of the colleges which came out of a revival-istic background would include many of the best known educational institutions in the country.[b] Oberlin College, perhaps the most richly endowed institution of college grade in America, furnishes an interesting example of the revivalistic influence in college founding. Charles G. Finney, its most famous president (1851–66), was one of the greatest of American revivalists, and under his leadership Oberlin became the most important revival centre in the nation. The list of colleges whose origins are related to revivalism would include every one of the most distinguished Baptist, Congregational, Methodist, and Presbyterian colleges today—and more than any other single influence it was the multi-plication of denominational colleges on the succession of American

[a] W. W. Sweet, *Revivalism in America: Its Origin, Growth, and Decline* (New York 1944). Chapter 8, 'Revivalism on the Wane', pp. 162–82.

[b] Donald G. Tewksbury, *The Founding of American Colleges and Universities before the Civil War, with particular reference to the religious influences bearing upon the College Movement* (New York 1932). W. W. Sweet, *Religion on the American Frontier*, Vol. II, *The Presbyterians*, Chapter 3, 'Cultural and Educational Influence of the Presbyterians in the Early West'. Also Peter G. Mode, *The Frontier Spirit in American Christianity* (New York 1923).

frontiers which accounts for the decentralizing and the democrat-
ization of higher education in America.[a]

The numerous reform movements which swept over the
English-speaking world in the early nineteenth century owed
much of its impetus to revivalism. The anti-slavery movement,
especially in its middle-western phase, was intimately related
to Finney revivalism. The new interest in Indian missions which
arose in the middle of the eighteenth century, and the formation of
the bewildering number of agencies of all kinds in the first half
of the last century particularly, to advance good causes of all
kinds, are all rooted in revivalism. Though many of these agencies
had no formal connexion with the Churches, yet they were all the
legitimate children of the revivalism of the time. The rise of
foreign missions to a place of predominant concern in American
Protestantism is likewise rooted in the revivals which swept the
nation in the early years of the last century, which reached their
culmination in the new type of revivalism, which was carried on
through the medium of college Y.M. and Y.W.C.A.s, a generation ago, resulting in literally thousands of students going forth
from the colleges and universities to every corner of the globe to
bring in the reign of Christ throughout the world.

There were other by-products of revivalism, however, which
have produced unfortunate consequences. Revivalism has been
one of the most divisive forces in American Protestantism and
has thus contributed more than its share to controversy. The
confusion and disorder which revivalism undoubtedly fostered,
especially in the frontier stage of our development, still persists
in the public worship of the revivalistic Churches, especially in the
rural areas. This is illustrated by the type of songs still used in
village and rural churches today throughout the country, and is
particularly true of those churches which do not have a churchly
tradition, and an historic ritual and hymnody.

[a] W. W. Sweet, *Revivalism in America*, Chapter 7, 'The By-products of Revivalism',
pp. 140–61.

CHAPTER FOUR

THE MULTIPLICITY OF DENOMINATIONS

IT HAS OFTEN been stated that the great number of religious denominations in the United States is a scandal. Nowhere else in the world is the body of Christ so divided. At the present time the number of independent religious bodies in the United States is placed at two hundred and fifty-six, with an inclusive church membership of 72,492,669. This means that more than half the total population of the nation are either communicants or nominal members of some religious body. Of these, some forty-four million are Protestants, something over twenty-three million are Roman Catholic, four million six hundred thousand are Jews, and nearly seven hundred thousand are Eastern Orthodox. These figures would seem to indicate that the United States is the largest Protestant country in the world, the largest Roman Catholic country in the world, and the largest Jewish country in the world. It is Protestantism, of course, which is responsible for the great multiplicity of denominations.

This religious diversity will not seem so distressing when the principal reasons for it are understood. There are many causes for this phenomenon, but it will be the purpose of this chapter to set forth only those which seem to be the most significant.

I

The population of the United States is made up of a cross section of all the civilized peoples of the world, the great majority of them drawn from Europe. From the beginning America has been a refuge for the distressed people of the world. While many have come because of religion, the great majority of them were attracted to the New World in the hope of securing greater economic security. Naturally, in the course of this long-continued migration the various peoples brought their religions with them. All the religious bodies found in the colonies were direct European transplantations. In eighteenth-century colonial New York there were to be found at least fourteen kinds of religious bodies. In colonial Pennsylvania there were as many, if not more, varieties.

The colonial German migration was particularly notable for its diverse religious complexion, while all the varieties of Presbyterians, found in Scotland and North Ireland were brought to the New World. The vast nineteenth- and twentieth-century immigration brought with it a much greater variety of religious bodies of the world. In other words, the United States has been in a sense the draining sink for the world's religious differences and divisions. There are today twenty kinds of Lutherans in the United States, besides several religious bodies which are rooted in Lutheranism, all of them direct transplantations from the Old World. Practically all the Eastern Orthodox Churches to be found in Christendom are represented in the city of Chicago alone, and most of the many linguistic divisions in Roman Catholicism, including the Uniat Churches, are to be found in our polyglot cities. Old World divisions are therefore basically responsible for the religious diversity to be found in the New World.

II

A second factor accounting for the multiplicity of American religious bodies is that there has been throughout our national history practically complete religious liberty. One of the proudest traditions which America possesses is that she has thrown wide her doors for all peoples who have suffered for conscience. Americans believe with John Locke that 'liberty of conscience is every man's natural right, and no one ought to be compelled in matters of religion either by law or force'. Diversity is one of the prices we pay in America for the complete freedom of religious expression which our tradition and laws allow. Most Americans hold that it is far better to have two hundred and fifty-six different religious bodies, all equal under the law, than to have an authoritarian and privileged Church, with all the rest merely tolerated. In fact, toleration is a hateful word to a free people, for it implies a privileged body and inequality.

One of the safeguards of religious liberty in America is the fact that there are no majority religions. Every one of the two hundred and fifty-six Churches and sects in the United States are minorities. Indeed, religious liberty was won in the United States by the combination of minorities. James Madison, often called the father of the American Constitution, was fond of quoting Voltaire's aphorism: 'If one religion were allowed in England, the government would possibly become arbitrary; if there were two the people would cut each other's throats; but as they are a multitude they all live happy and in peace.' To this Madison added: 'Security for civil rights must be the same as for religious rights; it consists in the one case in a multiplicity of interests and in the other in a multiplicity of sects.' So that it can be said truthfully that the multiplicity of religious expression which prevails in the United States has not been entirely fruitless; at least it has served and still serves the cause of religious freedom.

Religious persecutions and wars have all arisen out of a situation where there has been an established majority religion, with power to restrict and restrain minorities—and as far as I am aware no majority religious body has ever voluntarily surrendered its privileged position. For instance, in New England where Congregationalism was established by law, and where it enjoyed special privileges under the law, it was not until the minority religious groups, combining with the unchurched element in the population, gained a majority of votes in the elections that complete religious liberty was secured. In other words, religious liberty is undoubtedly more secure where all religious bodies are minorities, than it is in a situation where there is a majority religion. This is true even should the majority religion be Baptist, which holds as its first and greatest principle the complete separation of Church and State and full religious liberty. Human nature is such that when an organization can dominate and control, it generally controls even though theoretically it is opposed to such control. Thus in many communities in the South it is practically impossible to elect anyone but a Baptist to office, just as it is a rare thing for a non-Catholic to hold an office in Boston, where Catholics are in a large majority.

The Roman Catholic Church has a long record of many centuries, even down to our own time, during which it has refused to permit equality of religious expression wherever it had the power to do so. Indeed, the Catholic Church looks upon religious intolerance as a feature of the ideal State, since it maintains that error, which is Protestantism, ought not to have under the law the same right, as truth, which is Roman Catholicism. Therefore, if and when the Roman Catholic Church can secure control by becoming a majority religion it will then be compelled in the interest of truth to restrain and restrict all other Churches. Wherever Roman Catholicism secures dominance there you will have at least always the threat of religious intolerance; wherever the Roman Catholics are a minority there and there only do they give even lip service to complete religious liberty. Here is a valid justification for seeing to it that the Roman Catholics be kept a minority, not only in the United States, but throughout the world, if the great principle of complete religious liberty is to be maintained. To a certain extent that same thing may be said of all Churches. Majority religious bodies of all kinds whatsoever have contributed little to the cause of human freedom. I should rather have five minority Churches than two hundred and fifty-six minority bodies; but I should prefer two hundred and fifty-six minority Churches to one dominant majority body.

III

A third factor which has exercised powerful influence in dividing and redividing religious bodies and in producing the denominational confusion in the United States is the extreme individualism which was so characteristic of the American frontier. The American frontiers were to a large degree settled by individuals, although there were not a few instances where there were group settlements; but on the whole, religious and cultural institutions were left behind by the pioneers. In other words, people simply moved away from the old community influences of the older settled society. A society in motion always has difficulty in carrying its cultural roots with it. Or to put it in the words of Horace Bushnell: 'Transplanted to a new field, the emigrant race lose, of necessity, a considerable portion of that vital force which is the organic and preserving power of society.'

Professor H. Richard Niebuhr has pointed out that on the American frontier two influences combined to create a peculiar frontier religious attitude: one was the independent and fearless nature of the pioneers, more or less in rebellion against established order; the other was the fact that the people who settled the west were generally poor and 'accepted or produced anew many of the characteristics of the faith of the disinherited, for the psychology of the frontier corresponds in many respects to the psychology of the revolutionary poor'.[a]

Some of the ethical and psychological characteristics of the religion of the poor are emotional fervour, spontaneity of religious feeling and the rejection of abstract creeds and formal ritual.

[a] H. Richard Niebuhr, *The Social Sources of Denominationalism* (New York 1929), Chapter 6.

Another is the development of lay leadership and the stress placed upon the simple virtues, such as mutual helpfulness, rigorous honesty, equality, and sympathy. Such virtues were much appreciated on the American frontier and the Disciples of Christ arose and grew rapidly, largely under lay leadership, because its emphasis was upon the poor man's virtues. The astonishing success of the Baptists and the Methodists in the American west was due also to the fact that both met the ethical and psychological needs of the poor.

The poverty of the frontier, however, was a peculiar kind of poverty. First of all, it was not hopeless poverty. In fact, frontiersmen were men of boundless optimism, knowing full well that within a few years many of them would have an abundance of this world's goods, and practically all of them a comfortable competence. At least all looked forward to better things in this world, though there was always enough tragedy in their lives and the lives of others about them to make them continually aware of the transient nature of this life and the reality of the world to come. This helps explain the rapidity with which the Churches of the poor, such as the Methodist, the Baptist, and Disciples, were transformed into middle-class and upper-middle-class Churches, while they continued to stress the poor man's virtues.

The rise of Mormonism in the 1830's was a peculiar frontier phenomenon. It grew right out of the crude American frontier soil and could have come from nowhere else. The *Book of Mormon* purports to be the account of the origin of the American Indians, a frontier topic of perennial interest. It abounds in Scripture passages and is couched in Biblical form. It deals with matters of trivial information and everyday experience; indeed, such things constitute the principal themes of the book. When the manuscript was brought to the printer it was entirely without punctuation, and was replete with misspellings and errors in construction. Even in recent editions the *Book of Mormon* still abounds in grammatical errors. Nowhere in the book is there a mention of a city, for the prophet Joseph had never seen a city, and it is entirely void of all mention of music, both indications of its frontier origin. With the death of Joseph Smith, there were divisions in Mormonism created by ambitious leaders, some of which still persist. Mormonism has persisted and has grown immeasurably strong in spite of its crudity and bizarre origin because of its effective, highly centralized organization, and the stress it places upon the simple frontier virtues.

IV

Revivalism has been one of the most divisive forces in American religion. As has been noted, it caused controversy and division among the colonial Congregationalists and Presbyterians. It was also a cause of dissension among the Presbyterians on the frontier and gave rise to the Cumberland Presbyterian Church, which still persists in the South. Opposition to revivalism was a factor in the emergence of Universalism and Unitarianism, and since 1880 it has been a major factor in the rise of the welter of pentacostal and holiness bodies which during the depression years were the fastest-growing religious bodies in the United States.

The waning of the revivalistic emphasis in the large evangelical Churches, due to their changing economic and cultural status, has been one of the principal factors in creating new revivalistic sects. The Methodists and Baptists have been the principal feeders of these bodies, especially in the rural and mountain sections of the South. The doctrine of the 'second blessing' has found largest acceptance among those whose material blessings are meagre, as was true in the early history of Methodism both in England and America. As the Methodist and Baptist ministers became better educated and as their churches tended to become increasingly costly and luxurious, the inevitable result was that the poor people no longer felt at ease in worshipping with their more fortunate brethren. Nor did the college- and seminary-trained minister stress the poor man's doctrines, such as 'holiness', the 'second blessing', and premillennialism, for the stressing of these doctrines caused the prosperous to feel uncomfortable.

It was out of this background that the revivalistic sects arose, such as the two relative large and growing Churches of God, the Assemblies of God, the Pilgrim Holiness, the Church of the Nazarine, and the Pentacostal Assemblies of Jesus Christ, and numerous others. During the depression years many of these sects grew with astonishing rapidity. The Assemblies of God, for instance, which were founded in 1914, had in 1937 175,000 members and 3,470 churches. The Church of God with headquarters in Cleveland, Tennessee, increased by about 400 per cent. in the ten years from 1926 to 1937. Similar Churches have arisen among the Negroes, both in the rural South and in the Negro sections of the great cities. All of these sects carry on continuous revivals, and stress the necessity of conversion. Their members maintain high moral standards and total abstinence from harmful habits. As long as American society is constituted of such uneven social and cultural groups, these unfortunate class cleavages will continue.

V

The presence of the Negro in large numbers in the United States has been a fruitful cause of religious controversy and division among the American Churches. In the first place, the most far-reaching and persistent schisms that have taken place in American Protestantism were caused by slavery, and since the Civil War numerous independent Negro Churches have emerged. Today there are at least thirty-three Negro Churches, entirely separate and self-governing. Until emancipation there were no independent Negro Churches in the south, since the relatively small number of slave Church members worshipped in the Churches of their masters. Of the three great Churches which divided over slavery, the Presbyterians, the Baptists, and the Methodists, only the latter have succeeded in healing that schism, though there still persists a Negro problem, since in the new Methodist Church the Negroes have been set apart into a separate jurisdiction. It was only on that basis, however, that the Southern Methodists would have been willing to unite. It still remains for the three large Negro Methodist Churches, the African Methodist Episcopal, the African Methodist Episcopal Zion, and the Coloured Methodist Episcopal to be brought into the union.

Such have been the principal factors which have been responsible for the seeming confusion which exists in American Protestantism. Some of these divisions have been caused by sharp differences over doctrines and polity, but generally speaking a great majority have arisen, not out of bitter controversy, but out of social and cultural cleavage.

VI

After all is said that can be said in condemnation of what seems the absurd diversity of denominationalism in America, there is, after all, not as much diversity as appears on the surface and as the cold statistics would seem to indicate. Of the forty-four million Protestants in the United States more than thirty million are found in the eight largest denominational families, the Baptists,

Congregationalists, Disciples, Episcopalians, Lutherans, Methodists, Presbyterians, and Evangelical and Reformed. And these Churches have been gradually growing closer and closer together. A hundred years ago the cultural and social gulf dividing Methodists, Baptists, and Disciples from the Episcopalians, Congregationalists, and Presbyterians, especially in the eastern sections of the nation, seemed permanent and impassable. That gulf today has almost completely disappeared.

Although, as has been noted, the strong individualism developed on the frontier was a divisive force, yet, as Professor Carl Becker has pointed out, there was in the frontier type of individualism a certain uniformity, an absence of deep-seated differences —and the type of religious diversity produced on the frontier was a diversity underlaid with a certain uniformity which made possible a much larger unity of action than on the surface seemed possible. They were all united in a common struggle to save the vast new west; they were all engaged in fighting the common evils which were everywhere in evidence. It is not far wrong to say of the great evangelical Churches in America today that their diversity is underlaid with even a larger degree of uniformity than was to be found a hundred years ago.

The great variety of interdenominational organizations which sprang up in the early part of the last century, such as the American Bible Society, the American Tract Society, and the American Sunday School Union, are illustrations of the underlying unity of purpose among the Churches which has always been present. The great camp-meetings which were particularly in evidence on the frontier were, at least in the beginning, interdenominational; such was the Chautauqua Movement, a development from the camp-meeting which was at its peak in the early part of this century. The first Foreign Missionary Society, the American Board of Commissioners for Foreign Missions, organized in 1810 by the Congregationalists, soon became interdenominational (as did also the American Home Missionary Society, formed in 1826), and rendered valuable aid to the Scandinavian Lutherans in the west. The temperance and anti-slavery movements were interdenominational. The Anti-Saloon League characterized as the Church at work against the Saloon was a powerful interdenomination agency which for more than a generation put the fear of God into the politicians, and it can be done again if and when Protestant indignation can be again organized, and it is on the way.

Let us hope when it comes that it will call forth a wiser leadership and a higher emphasis.

The great American universities and colleges, many of which were Church foundations, as well as the State universities, have been powerful agencies in breaking down denominational barriers. The faculties and student bodies of all the most distinguished American institutions of learning represent a cross-section of the American Churches. None of the universities have any religious test for admission, though most of them list Church preferences for the benefit of the Churches serving the college or university community.

Not only is general education undenominational, but theological education is becoming increasingly so. Churches such as the Lutheran and Episcopalian are the only large denominations which maintain strictly denominational theological schools. The theological seminaries of the Methodists, Baptists, Presbyterians, Disciples, and Congregationalists are all to a greater or lesser degree interdenominational. The Divinity School of the University of Chicago, established by the Baptists as a part of the University of Chicago, had, during this last spring quarter, students from twenty-two denominations. For a number of years past the Methodists have had the largest student attendance of any of the Churches. The same thing is true of the Yale Divinity School and Union Theological Seminary in New York, where also Methodist students outnumber any other denominational group. Last year more than four hundred Methodist theological students were attending non-Methodist theological schools throughout the United States. It is probable that the Methodists are the most interdenominational of all the American Churches in this respect. As a matter of fact, a number of Methodist Conferences in the United States have officially accepted non-Methodist theological seminaries as acceptable training schools for the ministry. The faculties of the outstanding theological seminaries are also drawn from all the major denominations. The Chicago Theological Seminary, a Congregational institution, affiliated with the University of Chicago, has on its faculty men of Baptist, Disciple, Lutheran, Reformed, Presbyterian, and Methodist backgrounds; the same is true of the Divinity School of the University of Chicago, the Harvard and Yale Divinity Schools, Union Theological Seminary, and McCormick Theological Seminary, as well as numerous other seminaries less well known.

Religious and theological literature is likewise becoming increasingly interdenominational. The most influential interdenominational weekly journal in America today is the *Christian Century*, which developed out of a Disciple background. The *Christian Herald* is a popular interdenominational weekly that has circulated widely throughout the nation for many years. In more recent years such religious journals as *Christendom* and *Religion in Life*, both avowedly interdenominational, have been inaugurated, while the more scholarly journals such as *The Journal of Religion*, *The Harvard Theological Review*, *Church History*, and the reviews of the several Biblical societies are all widely interdenominational.

There are few, if any, of the major theological seminaries which do not offer courses in American Church History in which the total religious life of the nation is studied. This has made for a larger understanding among the Churches, and the breaking down of the walls which divide them. Such historical studies are leading to an increasing appreciation of all the religious forces which have helped to build American life and ideals. Also one of the results of a better educated ministry in all the Protestant Churches is the growing consciousness of the rich heritage which all the Churches share alike in the historic Church. In other words, the Protestant Churches are finding in the past a common standing ground; a new appreciation of the *Church* and the lessening emphasis upon 'the Churches'. They are beginning to realize that there is in the past a firm basis for union, and in the present a growing demand for it. The influence of this growing historic-mindedness in bringing about Church union is well illustrated by what happened in achieving the union of American Methodism in 1939. By that time the leaders in all the main branches of American Methodism had come to accept a common viewpoint on all the historic controversial issues over which they had divided. That did not mean that they had come to full agreement on all the old issues, nor that they were forgotten, but rather that they were now fully understood. Church union will come, not from disregarding past conflicts and differences, but out of an understanding of them.[a]

The fact that there are no privileged Churches in America has rendered such terms as *nonconformity* and *dissenter* meaningless. Nor is there any sharp distinction between *church* and *chapel*. In fact

---

[a] 'Rapprochement in American Protestantism', by W. W. Sweet, *Religion in Life*, Vol. XI (1941–2), pp. 74–83.

the Churches which were the privileged bodies in the colonial period, the Episcopalian and the Congregational, have suffered because of it. Both were handicapped by an upper-class attitude which is one of the reasons why neither of them have become numerous bodies, as compared to the great democratic Churches.

Thus by the recognition of equality under the law of all religious bodies in the United States one of the greatest barriers to cordiality between the Churches was removed. On the other hand, the long tradition of an established Church in England and Scotland has naturally created superiority and inferiority complexes and produced cleavages which no amount of good intentions can bridge.

The concept of the Church which has come to prevail in American Protestantism is that of a voluntary society, and not of an authoritarian institution tied to the State. Its sacraments are means of grace rather than symbols of historic confessions. The great historic confessions of faith from the Council of Nicea onward were often as much the result of political expediency as of the desire to advance religious truth. There have been but two instances in American history where the adoption of confessions of faith had political significance, and both came out of New England, where Congregationalism was established. The complete disestablishment which came about in America soon after independence has saved us from making creeds and confessions of faith political symbols. The complete disappearance of all legal inequalities creates a favourable atmosphere for the promotion of interchurch harmony and understanding.

We generally think of Church union in terms of interfaith conferences, formal resolutions, and declarations of ecclesiastical bodies, and seldom in terms of the real basic factors which must underlie them if anything is to be accomplished. While there has been much progress made in recent years in bringing about formal union between Protestant bodies in the United States—since 1906 there have been twelve Church unions accomplished—we have overlooked the gradual drawing together in closer fellowship and understanding of all the major Protestant bodies; and Church union must be a growing process.

CHAPTER FIVE

THE AMERICAN NEGRO AND HIS RELIGION

No PHASE OF American religious and Church life is more of an enigma to an outsider than the religion of the Negro and the part it plays in his own life and in the religious life of the nation.

In round numbers there are about fourteen million Negroes in the United States today, of which some ten million are in the southern states. About fifty per cent. of the total Negro population are members of Churches. The Negro Baptists are by far the most numerous, with over four million members; the three largest Negro Methodist churches, the African Methodist, the Zion, and the Coloured Methodist Episcopal, have a total membership of about one million seven hundred thousand, while in the predominantly white reunited Methodist Church there is a Negro membership of some three hundred thousand. Thus seven-eighths of the Negro Church membership in the United States is either Baptist or Methodist.

Not only has the Negro contributed to the denominational 'confusion of tongues' by adding thirty-three separate religious bodies to the list, but his presence has been the cause of the greatest and most far-reaching schisms that have ever occurred in American Protestantism.

Previous to emancipation there were no independent Negro Churches except in the North, where free Negroes began to form themselves into independent congregations in the early part of the last century. Previous to the Civil War all the slave states had outlawed Negro organizations of all kinds, prohibiting Negroes to assemble even for worship except under white supervision. It was fear of slave insurrection that prompted such restrictive measures. Little was attempted on the part of the southern Churches to give religious instruction to the slaves until a generation previous to the Civil War. The Methodists, however, from the beginning had adopted the policy of receiving Negroes into Church membership, and in 1830 there were 69,000 coloured members of the Methodist Episcopal Church. Negro members in Baptist Churches were also relatively numerous by 1830. It was the rise of the anti-slavery

D

movement, which merged into the Abolition movement, with its increasingly bitter denunciation of slavery and the sin of slave-holding, that stirred the southern Churches to greater activity, and by the opening of the Civil War there were more than 200,000 Negro members of the Methodist Church, South, and 150,000 Negro Baptists. The Negroes generally worshipped with the whites, being assigned to the galleries or the back seats of the churches. Plantation missions were also inaugurated under white direction, in which there was a certain amount of Negro leadership permitted.

It may come as a surprise to many to learn that the most responsible Christian leaders in the *ante-bellum* South never defended slavery as an ultimate good. They recognized it as an evil, brought into the world by the sin of our first parents, just as was poverty, disease, and death. In the world to come, they held, there would be no masters and slaves, just as there would be no poverty, disease, or death. These leaders recognized their obligation to the slave, considered them as persons, and insisted that the master was under obligation to have his servant taught his duties to God as well as his duties to man.[a] It is significant that on the formation of the Methodist Episcopal Church, South, in 1846, the rules on slavery were retained, declaring in answer to the question: 'What shall be done for the extirpation of the evil of slavery?'—'We declare that we are as much as ever convinced of the great evil of slavery.'

Contrary to the statement that is often made, the Negroes were not forced from the white Churches after their emancipation. Rather they generally left the white Churches of their own accord, since continuing to worship with their former masters and sitting in the galleries or the back pews was a constant reminder of their previous condition of servitude. Many free Negroes from the North came South following the war and soon were in positions of leadership. In a relatively short time all southern Negroes had withdrawn from the predominantly white Churches and were assisted by their white brethren in building churches and in securing an ordained ministry. Thus the Southern Methodists assisted in the formation of the Coloured Methodist Episcopal

[a] James H. Thornwell, Professor of Theology at the Presbyterian Theological Seminary at Columbia, South Carolina, 1855–62, produced the most effective theological pro-slavery arguments. See his 'Rights and Duties of Masters', a sermon preached before a Negro congregation in Charleston, South Carolina, in 1850 (*Southern Presbyterian Review*, July 1850, pp. 105ff.).

Church, and helped them to establish their schools and colleges.[a]

The northern Churches at the end of the war looked upon the *ante-bellum* South as a new mission field and were active in forming agencies to carry on educational work, particularly among the Negroes. As a result there are today numerous excellent Negro schools and colleges scattered throughout the former slave states, turning out an ever-increasing number of well-trained Negro leaders in every walk of life, an achievement in which the Churches may well take pride.[b]

As far as Church organization is concerned, the Negro has been largely an imitator of his white brethren, but the typical Negro's religion is something distinctive. His more than two hundred years of slavery not only furnished the slave a central theme for his religion, but to a large degree that central theme still persists. His religion today is still dominantly reminiscent of his long servitude, because he is fully aware that he is not yet completely free. In a recent study made of Negro preaching, it was found that over three-fourths of the sermons stenographically reported in urban Negro churches were of the other-worldly, Biblical types.[c] This was true to an even larger extent of rural preaching, and in only a relatively small number was there any attempt to apply Christianity to life. This throws light upon one of the principal weaknesses of the Negro's religion, his failure to see any close relationship between his religion and morality. The uneducated Negro minister is instinctively imaginative and dramatic and delights in the use of big and high-sounding terms, without bothering to understand or to define them. His conception of God is simple. God is a loving and forgiving Father and trusting in Him is a panacea for all ills. He deals out special favours for those who trust Him.

More distinctive than Negro preaching is the Negro spiritual, in which the central theme is often death and heaven. Dean Sperry has well stated that 'the Negro spirituals are perhaps our

---

[a] W. W. Sweet, 'Negro Churches in the South: A Phase of Reconstruction', *Methodist Review*, 1921, pp. 405–18. Also C. G. Woodson, *The History of the Negro Church*, Washington, 1921. For a discussion of the Negro withdrawal from the white Churches see Chapter 9, 'The Civil War and the Church'.

[b] Among the several Negro colleges and universities are Howard University in Washington, D.C., Clark University and Atlanta University; Fisk University, Tallidaga, Shaw, Rust, Philander Smith, Bennett colleges, while a number of the southern states have established separate state colleges for the training of Negroes. Negroes are admitted to most northern colleges and universities.

[c] Benjamin E. Mays and Joseph W. Nicholson, *The Negro's Church* (New York 1933) Chapter 4, 'The Message of the Minister'. See also p. 17.

most moving statement of an inescapable fact and a serene hope',[a] Such haunting phrases from the spirituals as:

> Deep river, deep river, Lawd,
> Deep river, Lawd, I want to cross over in a ca'm time,
> I want to meet death smilin',

or

> Swing low, sweet chariot,
> Coming for to carry me home,

find a universal response in all of our hearts. Or in such words as these, reminiscent of a time when, as barefooted slaves working in the cotton fields, they looked upon shoes as a luxury, only to be obtained in a world to come—

> I got-a shoes, an' you got-a shoes,
> All Gawd's chillun got-a shoes,
> An' w'en I git to heav'n, gon-a put on m-shoes
> An' walk all ovah Gawd's heav'n,
> Heav'n, heav'n, gon-a walk all ovah Gawd's heav'n,

is expressed a calm and confident self-possession in the presence of hardships and death which many of us, with our more sophisticated religion, cannot match.

Both spirituals and sermons reflect the idea of God as omnipotent, omnipresent, and omniscient. God is sovereign in both earth and heaven. God is just and will see to it that the wicked are destroyed, the righteous vindicated, and the heavy-laden given rest.

Rest comes after the burdens of this world are laid down. Heaven provides crowns, golden slippers, shoes, and robes. All these are symbols of the reward which Heaven brings to all who hold out to the end. God answers prayer and the one who faithfully prays will be rewarded in the end.[b]

The Church has meant more to the Negro than any other institution. The limits that have been placed upon his participation in the civic, political, and economic life of the nation have tended to magnify the importance of his Church. There he finds the chance fully to express himself[c]—and perhaps the principal reason why seven-eighths of the Negro Church members are

---

[a] Willard L. Sperry, *Religion in America* (Cambridge University Press 1945).
[b] Benjamin E. Mays, *The Negro's God* (Boston 1921).
[c] Mays and Nicholson, *The Negro's Church*, Chapter 1, 'The Church in Negro Life', pp. 1–18.

either Baptists or Methodists is because there is a larger opportunity for self-expression and lay leadership in these Churches than in others. The morning service of a Negro Baptist church in Chicago will have a dozen laymen taking part in the service; and it is not unusual for a large church to have three or even four choirs.

There is a growing body of Negro leaders, both in and out of the Churches, who are no longer willing to delay the possession of shoes and all that shoes typify until Heaven dawns. They want justice and a fair deal for the Negro here and now, and they are determined to get it, even at the expense of physical violence. In fact, the Negro problem in the United States today is about as explosive as the atomic bomb. It is encouraging to know that these demands that the Negro is making to become a full citizen of the United States are receiving increasing support from white leaders, in the Churches particularly, both in the South as well as in the North. The Negroes also have some very able leaders, many of whom have gained recognition in the realm of literature, art, and music especially, which gives hope for the future. The Negro chemist, George Washington Carver, when asked by a white man if he thought the Negro was as good as a white, answered: 'He is when he is.' Increasingly, the truth in that statement is coming home to the American people.

The situation of the Negro in the United States today is in many respects similar to that of the people of India. The Indian people for the past one hundred and fifty years have been in training for self-government under British tutelage. Excellent schools have been established under British direction from which have come many trained native leaders. The Indian people have been taught the meaning of British justice and the forms and procedures of self-government. But the British have been as reluctant to give them complete self-government as was Pharaoh in granting freedom to the Children of Israel. So likewise the Negro in the United States has been slowly but surely, in spite of many handicaps, preparing for full participation in the life of America. Excellent schools have been established out of which many distinguished Negro leaders have arisen. It is true that the Negro has been discriminated against in his struggle to secure an education, but there is no denying his rapid progress. Just as the people of India have a definite programme of demands, so also have the American Negroes, which in the interest of building a peaceful world must be honestly met. Listen to what one Negro has recently written: 'Negroes want to be accepted by our American society as citizens who in reality belong, who have the respect of their fellow men and equality of opportunity for life, liberty, and the pursuit of happiness. Negroes want what good men want in every democratic society. If they wanted less they would not deserve the status of citizens.'[a]

The Negro still looks to the white man and the white man's Church for example and assistance. He wants his own Church and his own leadership, but still feels dependent upon his white brethren for advice and support. This attitude of dependence on the part of the Negro Church leaders arouses resentment on the part of a growing number of Negro intellectuals many of whom have repudiated the Church and characterize this dependent attitude as 'Uncle Tomism'.

[a] Rayford W. Logan (editor), *What the Negro Wants* (Chapel Hill, University of North Carolina Press, 1944).

CHAPTER SIX

ROMAN CATHOLICISM IN THE UNITED STATES

AT THE END of the American War for Independence not more than one per cent. of the population of the new nation were Roman Catholics. There was one Catholic signatory of the Declaration of Independence, Charles Carroll of Maryland, the wealthiest man in that colony, but his importance was due to his wealth and social standing, and was in spite of his Catholicism rather than because of it. Throughout the eighteenth century Roman Catholics had been under legal disabilities in all the colonies, and it was only with independence that they secured the right to participate in government and enjoy the privileges of full citizenship.[a]

American Catholics in recent times have made large claims as to the part played by their co-religionists in winning independence and in the establishment of religious freedom, but outside Catholic circles these claims have been largely discredited on the basis of the lack of historic evidence. It is, however, but natural for a body, more or less recently come to power and influence, to desire to project its influence in the past, just as it is for the newly rich to desire to acquire a family tree.[b]

The swarming of Roman Catholics to the United States, from all the Catholic countries of the world, beginning with the great exodus from southern Ireland, due to the potato-rot famine and continuing until the outbreak of the First World War, has made the Roman Catholic Church the largest religious body in the United States, with an estimated membership of some twenty-three millions. This rapid increase in numerical strength has rendered them increasingly assertive and historically conscious. Since 1918 the American Catholic University in Washington, D.C., alone has sponsored more than fifty doctoral dissertations in American Catholic history, most of which are historically sound, though practically all have been censored by the Church.

[a] Sister Mary Augustana (Ray), *American Opinion of Roman Catholicism in the Eighteenth Century* (New York 1936), is an excellent study of the Catholic situation in the colonies.
[b] For a summary of such Catholic claims see Theodore Maynard, *The Story of American Catholicism* (New York 1941), especially Chapter 8, 'Catholics in the Revolution', and Chapter 9, 'Religious Liberty is won'.

This fact in the eyes of outside historians renders them somewhat suspect. For censored history must be classed as propaganda, even though it may display much sound scholarship.[a]

Though immigration has been the principal cause of the great increase in Catholic numbers, a secondary cause has been the large Catholic families. Although there are no accurate figures as to the number of converts from Protestanism to Catholicism, they have been relatively few. A Catholic source, Bishop Gerald Shaughnessy, estimates that from 1820 to 1920 there have been 883,000 converts. Of this number probably 250,000 are now living, which means that of the twenty-three millions of Catholics now in the United States, 22,750,000 are either immigrants or the descendants of Catholic immigrants.[b] Wide publicity has been given to conversions of Protestants to Catholicism in Catholic publications, especially when people of prominence embrace the Catholic faith.

As has been noted, the first great Catholic immigration was from southern Ireland, and by 1880 some four and a half million Irish had landed on American shores. Though in its beginning the most poverty-stricken, illiterate, and improvident immigration that ever set foot on American soil, in an astonishingly short time it had accommodated itself to its American environment, and it was not long before they considered themselves fully fledged Americans. A hundred per cent. Roman Catholic and without resources, the first Irish comers were compelled to settle down in cities along the Atlantic seaboard, where their genius for political plotting soon gave them control of city governments of many cities in the eastern section of the United States. It is the Irish political boss and his non-Irish Catholic constituency which must bear a large share of the blame for the corrupt political machines which have so long misgoverned many American cities. The fact that the Irish immigration was English-speaking and easily assimilable also gave the Irish the largest percentage of leadership in the Roman Catholic Church in the United States. The extent to

[a] John Paul Cadden, *The Historiography of the American Catholic Church, 1785–1943* (Washington, D.C., 1944). Monsignor Peter Guilday, Professor of American Church History in the Catholic University, has furnished much of the inspiration as well as direction for this renaissance in Catholic history writing. For an example of recent Catholic history writing, outside the dissertation type of study, see Robert H. Lord, John E. Sexton, Edward T. Harrington, *History of the Archdiocese of Boston, etc., 1604–1943*, 3 vols. (New York 1943). See my review of the above in *The American Historical Review*, Vol. L, No. 3 (April 1945), pp. 542–4.

[b] Gerald Shaughnessy, *Has the Immigrant Kept the Faith? A Study of Immigration and Catholic Growth, 1790–1920* (New York 1925).

which this is true is indicated by the fact that at least a hundred native Irish have occupied episcopal sees in the United States and twice that number of American-born Irish have been bishops—and the sees occupied by the Irish are the most important ones.

The New England States are today the most Catholic part of the country. Of the total population of New England, two-fifths are Roman Catholics, two-fifths unchurched, and only a little more than one-fifth are members of Protestant and Jewish congregations. In no large American city have the Catholics such complete control as in Boston, the cradle of American Puritanism.[a] A commentary on the political situation too often furthered by Catholic dominance is furnished by recent happenings in Boston. The present Mayor, a Catholic in good standing, was elected to office while under indictment by a Federal court for fraudulent use of the mails. Since that time he has been convicted in a Federal court, but that in no way seems to have diminished his popularity among his constituency.[b]

Between 1830 and the opening of the First World War some five millions of Germans came to the United States. At least a third of this immigration was Roman Catholic, while the other two-thirds was about equally divided between Lutherans and rationalists. The early German immigration settled in rural areas and greatly increased the number of Roman Catholics as well as Lutherans in the middle west, especially in the states of Missouri and Wisconsin. At the same time there was a large Scandinavian immigration into the middle western section of the United States which, of course, had a hundred per cent. of Lutheran complexion. This immigration we term the old immigration to distinguish it from the great inundation of immigrant people which has swept into the United States since 1880. The old immigration, with the exception of the Irish, settled largely in rural areas; the new immigration, coming mainly from southern and eastern Europe, became city dwellers. The mere listing of their numbers fills even an American with astonishment: 1,800,000 Czechs; 500,000 Slovaks; 3,400,000 Poles; 750,000 Russians; 500,000 Ukranians; 600,000 Hungarians; 1,640,000 Bulgarians, Lithuanians, and Latvians; 500,000 Greeks; 200,000 Armenians;

a See Lord, Sexton, Harrington, *History of the Archdiocese of Boston*, op. cit.
b Maynard, *The Story of American Catholicism*, pp. 506–7, has high praise for the Irish, and considers it providential that theirs should have been 'the guiding hands of the Church in the United States'.

50,000 Portuguese; five million Italians; a million and more Mexicans; besides Chinese and Japanese; and four million Jews from the four corners of the earth.

Of the newer immigration at least three-fifths was either Roman or Eastern Orthodox Catholic. From 1880 to 1910 Roman Catholicism added to their numbers in the United States more than five millions by immigration alone. There has been much resentment, especially among the Poles and Italian Catholics, over the continued Irish domination. This new immigration brought with it, of course, a vast confusion of tongues, together with a great variety of racial idiosyncrasies and Old-World peasant superstitions. There were also transplanted off-shoots of all the Uniat Churches of the world, with their differing rites and customs of worship. In 1930 in the city of Chicago alone there were 124 English Catholic churches, thirty-five German, twelve Italian, eight Czech, thirty-eight Polish, nine Lithuanian, ten Slovak, four Croatian, five French, and eight others, including Mexican and mixed.

Since this new immigration was so overwhelmingly Roman Catholic, the problems it posed were primarily Catholic ones. To shepherd these millions of souls, speaking thirty or more languages, with all their Old-World differences, presented a situation more intricate than that which has faced any other religious body in the modern world. In some respects, it was not unlike the problem faced by Baptists, Methodists and Presbyterians on the early frontier, since in both instances it was a matter of dealing with uprooted peoples.

It is easy to criticize Roman Catholic shortcomings in dealing with this situation, just as it is easy to sneer at the revivalism of the frontier Churches. But if there had been no Catholic Church in America, to restrain and control these teeming millions of foreign-speaking people, coming, as they did, mostly from the lower economic and cultural strata of European society, the American cities would have been far more lawless and crime-ridden than they are today. It was Protestantism which saved the restless and reckless frontier from sinking into barbarism; Catholicism was the largest factor in keeping the American cities from becoming veritable Sodoms and Gommorahs.

In contrast to English Roman Catholicism, which has always possessed a large aristocratic element, Catholicism in America has been largely made up of European peasants, or the descendants of Europe's peasantry, transplanted to the great American industrial cities. Here they still constitute insulated pockets of European peasant culture, with their own language, churches, and parochial schools, getting their news from their own language newspapers and broadcasts. Accustomed to living under European landlords, and dominated by a Catholicism in the Old World much more authoritative than that in the United States, they were easily amenable to political control in the great American cities, especially when led by clever Irish Catholic leaders. Unaccustomed to democratic processes, and with little knowledge of American history and institutions, the first generation of such immigrants became easy prey of corrupt political bosses. Basically, however, they are good material for American citizenship, are proud of being Americans, and are devoted to the great principle of freedom and opportunity for which America stands.

The mere listing of the facts and figures as to the immense and long-continued swarming of Roman Catholics from every country of Europe constitutes an explanation in itself for the emergence of anti-Catholic movements which have occurred periodically throughout the last century.[a] Indeed, it would have been strange if such outbreaks had not occurred. Even to-day a great majority of the American people still look upon the Roman Catholic Church as a foreign transplantation, that has never been acclimatized to the American political and cultural soil, and the general assumption among them is that it never will nor can become so. To most American non-Catholics, constituting at least five-sixths of the population of the United States, the Catholic is a mysterious stranger, at least as far as his religious life and activities are concerned. There is a mingling of Catholic laymen and his Protestant neighbours in the ordinary affairs of life; in business and community interests, and in carrying on the affairs of government, but when the Catholic crosses the threshold of his church he puts an almost impassable barrier between himself and his non-Catholic neighbours. The good Catholic never

[a] These anti-alien and anti-Catholic movements have been thoroughly studied and their causes are well understood by the American historian. See R. A. Billington, *The Protestant Crusade; 1800–60* (New York 1938); John M. Mecklin, *The Ku-Klux-Klan* (New York 1924). The Catholic writers, such as Maynard and Shaughnessy, treat them as outbreaks of Protestant bigotry, conveniently overlooking the much longer story of equally blind and violent Catholic resistance to Protestantism that has gone on in the past centuries and is still going on wherever *Roman Catholics* are in political control.

enters a Protestant church; in many instances he is forbidden to do so. The attempts now being made to promote fellowship between Jews, Protestants, and Catholics has gained relatively small support from Catholics.[a] For a Catholic any 'process of adjustment conference, organization, or reconciliation . . . between the point of view of different Churches is something entirely out of agreement with his concept of unity of the Church itself'. In other words, for the Catholic, his Church is within itself a perfect unity and any attempt to compromise or adjust to any other Church, instead of creating a larger unity, only serves to destroy the unity within what he considers the only true Church.

Catholics would take strong exception to any statement or implication that Roman Catholicism is out of harmony with American political and social ideals, or that it is not thoroughly at home on American soil. The American Catholic hierarchy from John Carroll, the first American bishop, through bishops John England, John Hughes, John Ireland, and Cardinal Gibbons, to name only a few of the great leaders of the past, to the present Cardinal Spellman, have insisted that the Catholic Church in America has always been thoroughly in accord with American democratic principles and indeed has led the way in the march toward a more perfect democracy and religious freedom.

Cardinal Gibbons and Archbishop Ireland insisted that it was necessary to have as bishops men in accord with American ideals, and frequently spoke in favourable terms of the prevailing religious liberty in the United States. These American Irish bishops, however, have been embarrassed on numerous occasions by denunciations from Rome of the heresy of Americanism. The Syllabus of Errors of Pope Pius the Ninth (1864), generally accepted by Catholics as an infallible utterance of the Supreme Pontiff, cut sharply across American principles, especially in its condemnation of all public education not under the control of the Roman Catholic Church. Also the encyclical of Pope Leo the Thirteenth, condemning the separation of Church and State and religious liberty as it exists in the United States, are instances of official Roman Catholic condemnation of basic American principles. Some Catholics, as Cardinal Newman, for instance, have

[a] An explanation of the Catholic position on co-operation is clearly set forth by John LeFarge, 'Roman Catholicism', Chapter 2, W. L. Sperry (editor), *Religion and our Divided Denominations* (Cambridge, Mass., 1945).

held that neither of these papal pronouncements are binding, since the Popes were not speaking *ex cathedra*, and are therefore simply pronouncements of Papal opinion and policy. Whether or not this is true, the hierarchy in the United States have pretty generally accepted them in principle. At the same time, they accept for the present the separation of Church and State, as giving them the best obtainable conditions under which Catholicism can carry on, but they consider it by no means a final solution.

These Papal pronouncements of the latter years of the last century put an end to the Americanizing trends among the Roman Catholic American prelates, and there have been no liberal American bishops and Archbishops fraternizing with their non-Catholic brethren since. To quote my colleague Dr. W. E. Garrison:[a]

'No more serious error can be made in judging of the spirit, the attitudes, and the methods of Roman Catholicism in the United States at the present time than the assumption that it has been permeated and transformed in some subtle fashion by the spirit of American institutions. There may have been some justification for such an opinion thirty years ago. There is none now. That individual laymen exhibit modern attitudes is of course true. But the attitude of the hierarchy, the "teaching Church", is unchangingly medieval, and the pressure of this hierarchy is exercised without cessation upon all laymen—except when some specific object is to be attained by allowing the liberal utterance of a layman—such as Al Smith in the presidential campaign of 1928—to go temporarily unrebuked.'

The hundred per cent. support of Franco on the part of the American hierarchy and their bitter opposition to Protestant missions in South America are further proof, if further proof is needed, that the American prelates only accept religious liberty where Catholics are in the minority, but hold to a policy of intolerance of other faiths in countries where Catholics are in the majority. The Papal campaign against Communism finds unanimous support among the American hierarchy and pretty generally also among the 'mine-run' of American Catholic laymen. Claiming to champion the cause of Christianity against godless Communism, they are bidding for the support of the American people as a whole in their fight against Russia. On the whole,

[a] *Catholicism and the American Mind*, p. 243.

however, non-Catholics in the United States seem wary of giving support to such a campaign, many holding that Roman Catholicism is as inimical as is Communism to our basic freedoms because of its reactionary nature and its tie-up with Fascism. What has happened and is happening in Spain and Argentina and the official Roman Catholic attitudes toward these Fascist sore spots has been too widely publicized for the American people to give support to any Roman Catholic programme for world control.

Roman Catholicism has made some distinct contributions to American life and culture. One such contribution is the example they have set in emphasizing the habit of worship. There is no doubt but that Catholics go to church more faithfully than do American Protestants—and they go to church to worship, never to be merely entertained, or hear a sermon. Nor do they go to church to meet their friends. Unlike many American Protestant churches, Roman Catholic churches are not social units, and the social emphasis in worship is therefore much less emphasized than among Protestants.

Catholic worship is largely symbolized, while Protestant worship consists largely of the sermon and congregational participation, tending to bring everything down to man's understanding. Catholic worship promotes the spirit of trust in the unseen, the mysterious and supernatural. Catholics are taught to utilize intangible aids, which say things to them that words cannot convey.

Catholics have taken the lead in promoting charities, especially in our great cities. In the building and maintaining of hospitals they have performed a notable service, and their example has been largely responsible for the greatly expanding hospital movement in all the major Protestant bodies.

It has already been noted that the authority exercised by the Catholic Church in America over the swarming Catholic immigrants has been a large factor in their Americanization and control.

A number of factors have been responsible for worsening relationships between Protestantism and Roman Catholicism in America in recent years. There has always been a strong undercurrent of anti-Catholic feeling in America, often manifesting itself in crude outbreaks such as that of the Ku-Klux-Klan in the 1920's. But the rising tide of resentment against Roman

Catholicism today, however, cannot be classed with these earlier outbreaks. The most thoughtful and well-informed leadership in American Protestantism is becoming increasingly concerned about Catholic political pressure exerted in world affairs, especially since it is becoming quite apparent that the Roman Catholic hierarchy are aiming at a kind of world domination, inimical to the basic freedom of all our freedoms, religious liberty. The appointment by the President of the United States of a personal ambassador to the Vatican has been almost universally condemned by American Protestant opinion, on the constitutional ground that it is a violation of the American principle of the complete separation of Church and State. Also the anti-Russian propaganda endlessly carried on in the American Roman Catholic Press and elsewhere has aroused concern on the part of many thoughtful people because it has undoubtedly increased the difficulty of reaching any satisfactory international world adjustment which is so necessary now for the building of a peaceful world.

See articles in *Christianity and Crisis*, Vol. V, No. 2, 19th February 1945, 'Emergent Clericalism', by John A. Mackay; and Vol. VI, No. 9, 'The Protestant-Catholic Issue', by John D. Burnett.

CHAPTER SEVEN

ACTIVISM IN THE AMERICAN TRADITION

A COMMON generalization, more or less accepted without question in theological circles, is that American Christianity has been weak in theology, but strong in action. European theological scholars particularly seem to be unanimous in expressing contempt for what they consider our feeble theological efforts, as well as for our unashamed activism. Many of our American contemporary theologians are in full agreement with their European contemporaries in their estimate of us. Such estimates are at least partly due to a complete ignorance, on the part of both contemporary European and American theologians, of the history of American Christian thought.[a] Also the more or less servile dependence of our contemporary theologians upon European leadership, even more in recent years than formerly, and the failure of their theology to reflect American developments, has been another reason for this unfavourable opinion. In fact, during the last generation much of American theology as well as our theologians have been imported from the Old World.

As Dean Sperry has aptly put it, 'We Americans are predominantly the sons of Martha',[b] for, like Martha, we have been cumbered about with much serving. We refuse to admit, however, that the sons of Martha are any the less worthy than are the sons of Mary, even though a general assumption seems to be abroad that the Maryites are somehow superior to the Marthaites and have made a much more worthy contribution to historic Christianity.

Kipling's tribute to the Sons of Martha finds here an appropriate place:

They say to the mountains, 'Be ye removed'. They say to the lesser floods,
'Be dry'.
Under their rods are the rocks reproved—they are not afraid of that which
is high.

---

[a] Only in recent years has there been any interest in American Christian thought in our universities, and this has not been due to our theologians, but to men working in the field of American literature. Perry Miller's *Orthodoxy in Massachusetts* (Cambridge 1933), and his *The New England Mind* (New York 1939) are examples.
[b] Willard L. Sperry, *Religion in America* (Cambridge, England, 1945), p. 134.

Then do the hill-tops shake to the summit—then is the bed of the deep laid bare.
That the sons of Mary may overcome it, pleasantly sleeping and unaware.

Not as a ladder from earth to Heaven, not as a witness to any creed,
But simple service simply given to their own kind in their common need.

Both quietism and activism when carried to an extreme are
self-defeating. To push one or the other of these aspects of our
religion to the limit makes of religion either a passive and fatalistic
quietism on the one hand or a pure activism on the other, which
tends to identify God with finite forces, and results in bringing
God down to man's size. The pure quietist does nothing to make
a better world, because he conceives of God as determining all
and doing all; his becomes an attitude of complete passivity. On
the other hand, the pure activist tries like Atlas to bear the world
upon his own shoulders.[a] To a quietist, God is completely transcendent; to an activist, God is identified with man and walks the
earth. As Rudolph Eucken has stated, a religion which empha-
sizes the 'nothingness of man' is bound to result in giving religion
a character of passivity, of drowsy devotion, and of blind obedience; it threatens 'to take away all backbone out of life and to
transform it into mere sentimentality, weakness and dejection'.[b]
Such a religion becomes merely a set of highly abstract conceptions and loses all living content. God is a God of love—yes; but
it is a creative love, not something simply to be passively received.
He is a God of righteousness; but it is righteousness in action. He
is a God of justice; but also creating an order of justice in the
world. As Professor Hocking insists, we cannot choose between
'quietism' and 'activism'. We must choose both.[c]

No one has expressed more succinctly the common-sense position relative to the relationship between activism and quietism
than has Francis Asbury, who in 1779, at a time when his 'going
about doing good' had come under sharp criticism from the
Calvinists, noted in his *Journal*: 'We should so work as if we were
saved by the proper merits of our works; and so rely on Jesus
Christ to be saved by His merits and the assistance of His Holy
Spirit, as if we did no works. . . . What God hath joined together,
men must not put asunder.'

[a] H. F. Rall, *Christianity, An Inquiry into Its Nature and Truth* (New York 1940), pp.
32–40.
[b] Rudolph Eucken, *The Truth of Religion* (translated by W. T. Jones, New York
1911), pp. 579–81.
[c] W. E. Hocking, *The Meaning of God in Human Experience*, p. 427.

E

Here it is well to recognize the fact that the Church in America in these crucial times is suffering because in all too many instances a spring of action is wanting. We have been so busy going about doing good that we have had neither the time nor inclination to humbly seek that source of strength and power which can come only from an abiding faith and confidence in the Eternal. We call great meetings to talk of the necessity of mobilizing our spiritual forces, to meet the overwhelming problems which face us all in this troubled world, and too often we find that our spiritual health is frail and inadequate for the task. On the other hand, the quietism of the German Churches led them to accept, in too many instances, with little or no protest, the hideous Nazi régime, so they too found their spiritual resources in meeting their problems pathetically inadequate. If American activism cries out for a God-derived dynamic, European quietism needs to come down to earth and put its spiritual resources to work.[a] On the Sunday following the re-arrest of Pastor Niemoeller, the preacher of the day told the Dahlem congregation that there was but one thing a Christian could do in that crisis, and that was simply to 'watch and pray'. There was no suggestion that the hour required any concrete action. The Church had only spiritual weapons and Christians in the face of the most terrible injustices and cruelties must only watch and pray lest they fall into the temptation of losing their faith.[b] Such a do-nothing faith leaves American activists aghast, and, I fear, arouses something like contempt for such a spineless religion.

I

ACTIVISM AND PIONEERING

The American emphasis upon the application of Christianity to life has arisen out of certain definite historic factors. In the process of laying the foundations of Christian civilization in the New World something more than a passive faith was necessary. Much the same pattern of development which we find in the establishment of the primitive Church was followed in laying the foundations of the American Churches. Of necessity in both instances the stress was upon life rather than upon creed. The Apostles, in fact, might well be termed the first activists, for they were primarily concerned about winning men to the Christian

[a] *Christendom, An Ecumenical Review*, Vol. VIII (1943), No. 2. Article by Carl E. Schneider, 'German Quietism and American Activism', pp. 155–67.
[b] ibid., 157–8.

way of life. The Apostle Paul, upon whose writings so much of Christian theology is based, was first and last a missionary and his theology grew out of concrete experiences. Paul's theology is found in pastoral letters in which he was dealing with concrete problems and his primary interest was not intellectual. In the words of Dr. H. F. Rall: 'he was not a philosopher in search of the truth but a deeply religious man in search of life.'[a] So too the builders of the Church in America were deeply religious men bent upon bringing Christianity to bear upon life.

The Puritan emphasis upon 'dutiful living and its activist conception of God, nurtured a social tradition in which work was esteemed as the essential element in life'.[b] To the New England Puritans theology was far more than an exercise in dialectics; rather it was a matter of prime importance in their everyday lives.

The Puritans who settled New England were middle-class Englishmen engaged in the practical task of forming Christian communities in the New World. Their theology was not original with them, it was inherited and transplanted. It was in the application of theology to the practical task in which they were engaged that New England Puritanism made its unique contribution. The New Englander was primarily a doer of the word; the end of his theology was action. There was so much which demanded to be done, to do it at once was every Christian's first duty. Young men studying for the ministry were taught that 'divinity was not a speculative discipline but a practical one'. Thomas Hooker, perhaps the most eloquent of New England ministers of the first generation, was impatient of metaphysical argument, stating that 'while we are parlying and disputing what we should do, we omit so long to do what we ought, and unfit ourselves to do what we intend'.[c]

Though emphasizing the fact that the end of theology was action, the Puritans repudiated with all their might the Catholic doctrine that salvation came as a reward for good works. However important morality and work were in their eyes, they considered these things secondary to regeneration, which was entirely the work of God. A moral life and good works were useless if there was no regeneration. Good works and a moral life are

[a] H. F. Rall, *According to Paul* (New York 1944), pp. 6–7.
[b] H. Richard Niebuhr, *The Social Sources of Denominationalism* (New York 1929), pp. 83ff., 96, 203–5.
[c] Perry Miller, *The New England Mind* (New York 1939), pp. 47–9.

simply the outward manifestations of what had taken place in the heart. When in later generations the New Englanders sought to stress high ethical living without insisting upon a conversion experience they no longer were Puritans.[a]

Such studies as those of Max Weber and Troeltsch have tried to show that Calvinistic teaching had a distinct bearing upon the emergence of the middle class to economic importance, and upon the rise of capitalism. But if New England piety and economic success went hand in hand, it was not due to any deliberate plotting on the part of the New England Puritans for material advantage. Rather it came about as a natural consequence of the Puritan doctrine of 'calling'; that is, they held that a person is as divinely called to be a Christian merchant, or a Christian sea captain, or a Christian farmer as is one divinely called to enter the ministry. This emphasis of course lent itself to business success, and as a consequence New England prospered. For the very same qualities which made for the Christian life, as honesty, sobriety, moderation, faithfulness, made also for economic prosperity. Colonial New England prospered, in spite of its stony soil and inhospitable climate, largely because Puritan ethics and the Puritan way of life produced a type of men and women who had a holy concern for the training of children, the well-being of the family, of the Church, and of the commonwealth, as well as of the everyday concerns of making a living. New England Puritanism was an experiment in Christian living, in which the attempt was made to apply Christian principles to every phase of everyday life. Though their plan of government and social control failed, and it deserved to fail because of its intolerance and exclusiveness, yet Puritanism made rich contributions to American life particularly in the realm of personal character. We think of the Puritans as sturdy, honest, reliable, and industrious people concerned about every phase of human life. As a consequence of these qualities they have produced far more than their share of the intellectual, literary, educational, reform, and religious leadership in the nation.

II

ACTIVISM IN AMERICAN THEOLOGY: THE CALVINISTIC STRAIN

While New Englanders were the most theologically minded of all the colonists, there was not produced a mind among them capable

[a] Perry Miller, *The New England Mind* (New York 1939), p. 49.

of sustained independent speculation until Jonathan Edwards appeared at the end of the first third of the eighteenth century. It was the great New England awakenings which spurred him to become a theologian, and all of his great theological treatises are based in large measure upon his observations of what he saw happening to people in the course of the revival. His treatise on *Religious Affections*, which was a penetrating study of the place of emotion in religion, might well be called the beginning of the psychology of religion, though of course psychology had not at that time become a recognized science.[a]

The New England theology initiated by Jonathan Edwards, which constitutes a new chapter in the history of Christian thought, was carried on and developed through several generations of New England ministers. Of these Joseph Bellamy, Samuel Hopkins, Nathaniel W. Taylor, Horace Hushnell, and Charles G. Finney are the most significant. All of them were engaged in the practical work of the ministry. In fact, America has not produced a single cloistered theologian until relatively recent years. All the early American theologians were 'constantly solicitous for the practical usefulness of every theological theory' which they advanced. In other words, all of them were continually faced with the practical problem of applying their theology to life.[b]

Perhaps no theological emphasis in modern times has been responsible for more Christian activity than the 'disinterested benevolence' emphasis which was suggested by Jonathan Edwards, was given a central place in the Hopkinsian system, and came to full fruition in the New Haven theology of Nathaniel W. Taylor and the Oberlin theology of Charles G. Finney. In fact, here we find one of the principal strands of influence which has produced the Social Gospel emphasis in American Protestantism.

Samuel Hopkins was the first American to produce a system of theology. In this system he stressed disinterested benevolence as the supreme Christian motive. This emphasis naturally led to a conception of a universe steadily moving toward the greatest happiness of all mankind. The spiritual grandeur of such a

[a] A. C. McGiffert, *Jonathan Edwards* (New York 1932), a relatively recent study, calls attention in numerous places to Edwards' 'scent for facts' (p. 174) and that his theological treatises had a close tie with that life about him. His was no cloistered speculation.

[b] For the effect of Charles G. Finney's influence upon the anti-slavery movement and on the other reform movements of the first half of the last century see *The Anti-Slavery Impulse*, by Gilbert H. Barnes.

conception was a principal factor in inspiring succeeding generations of young men and women in New England to devote their lives to the righting of the world's wrongs. It is not strange to learn, therefore, that Samuel Hopkins himself was the first New England minister to take firm stand against slavery and the slave trade, and was the leader in a movement to send Christian American Negroes to Africa to begin the Christianization of the Dark Continent.

Edwards, Hopkins, Taylor, and Finney all stressed God's love for being in general, and that the highest good of the whole was God's design in creating the world. Since this is true, the highest good of the greatest number of God's creatures ought to be the chief concern of the Christian. This implied the need of spreading the Christian Gospel over the whole world. Suffering humanity, wherever it existed in the world, was a constant challenge to the 'disinterested benevolence' of the Christian. It was this doctrine of modified New England Calvinism which made Yale College, and the other New England colleges and theological seminaries of the early nineteenth century, the training centres for literally hundreds of young men, enthusiastic, devoted, and self-sacrificing, who directed their lives into every phase of Christian benevolence. They became missionaries to the American frontiers: they undertook foreign missionary work, and brought into existence the first American missionary agencies, the American Board of Commissioners for Foreign Missions in 1810 and a host of earlier home missionary societies. They went out to become college founders in the west; they established Bible and tract distributing agencies, to place the Bible and Christian literature in every home. They fought valiantly against drunkenness and formed temperance societies; they followed the example of Samuel Hopkins and became sturdy agitators against Negro slavery, and were not only anti-everything-wrong agitators, but were led to take an active part in government to right the wrongs of mankind, all of which they carried on for the greater glory of God.

Timothy Dwight,[a] the grandson of Jonathan Edwards and President of Yale College from 1795 to his death in 1817, furnishes a good example of the practical application of theology to life. He saw little good in purely metaphysical speculation and always avoided technical theological jargon, preferring always to express

[a] Charles E. Cunningham, *Timothy Dwight, 1757–1817* (New York 1942), pp. 319, 327–8.

himself in simple language. In doctrinal matters he kept his feet on the ground, and he thought of doctrine only in terms of its practical use. He had no liking for doctrinal controversy, using his influence to allay theological strife between religious groups. He thought of theology as something to be used in the pulpit, and that could be understood by the people who sat in the pews— and it was as a preacher that he tried out his theology. His appeal was both to the mind and the emotions, and because it was effective his *Theology: Explained and Defended* (in four volumes) went through many editions on both sides of the Atlantic. His was a common-sense theology, a combination of 'dependence upon God and personal responsibility'. During his administration of a little more than twenty years he transformed Yale College from a hotbed of Deism and religious indifference into a training school for missionaries, reformers, and Christian leaders in every walk of life. Yale College took on a national significance which it had never before possessed. John C. Calhoun is credited with the statement that he could recall the time when the natives of Connecticut, together with the graduates of Yale College, came within five of making a majority in Congress, which meant that Yale influence had spread throughout the newer sections of the nation.[a]

The first professor of theology in the Yale Divinity school, established in 1822, was Nathaniel W. Taylor, who became the founder of a school of thought known as Taylorism or the New Haven Theology. Though remaining within the framework of Calvinism, Taylorism radically reframed the old Calvinistic concepts in the interest of making it into a practical revivalistic theology. Like Edwards, Hopkins, and Dwight, Taylor was a preacher theologian, his primary concern being to develop a system of thought that could be preached effectively and for the purpose of bringing sinners to repentance. Before becoming a professor of theology he had been the minister of Centre Church, New Haven, and both as a preacher and a teacher the conversion of sinners, to his mind, outweighed every other consideration.[b] One of the characteristics of Taylor and those who accepted his theological leadership was the supreme confidence he had in the power of what he called 'Gospel doctrine', and the stress placed on human freedom and individual responsibility.

[a] F. J. Turner, *The United States, 1830–50* (New York 1935), p. 49.
[b] S. E. Mead, *Nathaniel William Taylor, 1716–1858, and the New Haven Theology*; Ph.D. thesis (typescript) (University of Chicago 1940), Chapter 10.

As a natural result of Taylor's concern for an effective preachable revivalistic theology the young men entering the ministry under his influence went forth imbued not only with his liberalized Calvinism but with his indomitable and confident spirit. Taylor's repudiation of inherited guilt and his insistence that 'sin consists in sinning' aroused a storm of controversy both within Congregationalism and Presbyterianism, which led finally to the formation of the New School Presbyterians into a separate body. The greatest preaching in the early half of the nineteenth century was by the exponents of Taylor's views, among the most eloquent being Lyman Beecher, Albert Barnes, and Charles G. Finney.

No theology or preaching in America ever brought about such far-reaching practical results as did that of Charles G. Finney. Accepting the Edwardian and Hopkinsian idea that 'all sin consists in Selfishness; and all holiness or virtue in disinterested benevolence', Finney's theology stressed the principal points in the New Haven theology and he preached them with thrilling effectiveness. Though holding that conversion was no miracle, but rather a result of the right use of constituted means, he nevertheless admitted the necessity of emotion in the converting process, stating that 'mankind will not act until they are excited' and that selfish people 'will never relinquish their selfish schemes until they are so excited that they cannot contain themselves'. Finney made salvation the beginning of religious experience in contrast to the older revivalism which made conversion the end. To him conversion was not an escape from life, but rather the beginning of new interests in life and in the building of God's kingdom. The net result of Finney revivalism which swept over the north from Boston on the east to Oberlin on the west like a tidal wave in the 'thirties and 'forties was to release a mighty impulse toward social reform. Calvinism was transformed into a practical affair adapted to American needs which encouraged men to work as well as to believe.[a]

The most spectacular direct influence coming out of Finney theology and Finney revivalism was the new anti-slavery impulse fathered by Theodore Dwight Weld, a Finney convert, who started an anti-slavery crusade, following Finney's revival methods. Unlike Garrisonian abolitionism, this new anti-slavery movement worked through the Churches, and was directly responsible for

[a] Charles G. Finney, *Lectures on Revivals* (New York 1835), pp. 10–12; quoted in G. H. Barnes, *Anti-Slavery Impulse*, pp. 10–11.

the sending of the first abolition members to Congress and for the writing of Harriet Beecher Stowe's *Uncle Tom's Cabin.*[a]

Horace Bushnell, a student of Taylor's, though never a disciple, belongs to the same generation as Finney and Lyman Beecher and in many respects was not only the most remarkable American preacher of his time, but as a preacher-theologian he exercised an influence on both sides of the Atlantic which still continues. Taylor's attempt to stay within the theological framework of Calvinism, even as a student, left Bushnell cold. There was too much logic and too little life in it to suit him, and accordingly he, from the beginning, threw Calvinism overboard. Bushnell had learned to look for truth from other sources and by other methods. As a result he became an intuitive searcher after divine truth. From the beginning of his ministry at North Church, Hartford, Connecticut, the only church he ever served, Bushnell was an accomplished preacher. Indeed, one of his early sermons, 'Every Man's Life a Plan of God', has been pronounced one of the greatest sermons of modern times. Though at the very time he began his ministry the Old School-New School controversy was raging, in which there was much splitting of theological hairs, he was not one to divide his hearers into theological parties. Rather his preaching transcended such squabbles, for he introduced his hearers into a world of life and experience. He believed that God was in His world and that heavenly grace comes into human life in the 'common ray of daily sunshine as well as in the lightning flash'. He challenged that conception of religion as having a compartment all to itself in our lives, as being wholly a separate interest from other affairs. Such a conception, he declared, was sure to issue in a defective morality.[b]

Bushnell developed no theological system; he had therefore no theological position to defend, which helps to explain why he was always a learner and always open-minded. He substituted a theology of experience and faith for a 'cold logical system which had little to do with life or with common sense'. He rescued Christ from being little more than a theological concept to a living, pulsing, appealing personality.[c] The Bushnell emphasis, as might be expected, produced a whole galaxy of followers,

[a] This whole story is magnificently told in G. H. Barnes' *Anti-Slavery Impulse, 1830–44* (New York 1933). For Finney's theology see his *Lectures on Systematic Theology* (ed. J. H. Fairchild, Oberlin, Ohio, 1887).

[b] Horace Bushnell, *Nature and the Supernatural* (New York), p. 244.

[c] John W. Buckham, *Progressive Religious Thought in America* (Boston 1919), Chapter 1, 'Horace Bushnell and the Liberators', pp. 3–52.

many of them some of America's greatest preachers—Theodore
T. Munger, George A. Gordon, Phillips Brooks, Washington
Gladden, and Newman Smyth, to name only a few among a
much larger number who belong in this noble company. Their
greatness lay in the fact that they all related religion to life, and
among them were those who were trail blazers in the Social Gospel
movement.

III

ACTIVISM: THE ARMINIAN STRAIN

We have been following the course of modified Calvinism and
have noted how, from Jonathan Edwards to Washington Gladden,
it tended to become increasingly activistic and practical in its
tendencies. Let us now consider another stream of influence in
American life, the Arminian.

Calvinism was triumphant in America throughout the colonial
period. Indeed, colonial revivalism was predominantly Calvinistic and generally speaking made only a limited appeal. If there
is such a thing, it was an aristocratic revivalism. It was not
until toward the end of the eighteenth and the beginning of the
nineteenth century that Arminian influence began to play much
of a part in the American religious scene. This was due to the
introduction and rapid development of Methodism; the rise of the
Free-will Baptists; the watering down of Calvinism among the
great majority of frontier Baptists; the emphasis on human worth
in the rising Unitarian and Universalist movements and the
beginning of the Campbell and Stoneite movements on the
frontier which eventuated into the Church of the Disciples.
Democratic individualism, as held by the Jeffersonian party, was
sweeping the country in the early part of the nineteenth century
and naturally found support in the popular religious movements
especially in the west.

Arminianism, with its emphasis on man's participation in his
own salvation, would naturally be more at home in a frontier
society than predestinarian Calvinism, which stressed man's
impotence and inability to do anything about his eternal welfare.
The doctrine that all men are equal in the sight of God and that a
plan of salvation has been provided for all, which man may accept
or reject, as he wills, was a much easier doctrine for the common
man to comprehend and accept than a doctrine which divided
men into rigid classes and limited salvation to the few.

The type of Arminianism which gained headway in seventeenth- and eighteenth-century England had rationalistic tendencies, depreciated the serious nature of sin, was indifferent to vital piety, and tended to encourage laxity in morals. It was this type of Arminianism against which Jonathan Edwards was inveighing when he began to preach his sermons on justification by faith, which brought on the great New England revival. It goes without saying that this was not the kind of Arminianism which John Wesley accepted and into which he breathed a profound and lofty spirit. More, perhaps, than any other single influence, Arminianism, with its emphasis upon the necessity of the co-operation of man with God in making a better world as well as a better life, has thoroughly leavened the Christian thought in America.

Arminianism, unlike Calvinism, never developed into a hard and fast credal statement, and never became the rigid theology of a denomination. Its very nature would prevent its becoming so. That is one of the reasons which caused those who accepted the Arminian position to become the advocates of a larger tolerance. In other words, it built no theological fences either to keep men in or out. It was, in fact, much more of a spirit than a creed; a state of mind rather than a rigid theological position; a permeating influence and not a theological club.

Arminianism became more naturally the theology of the common man, since its principal tenets tuned with his Christian experience. The 'practical man' dislikes 'dogmatic subtlety and philosophical abstraction' because it leads to 'unfruitful and theoretical discussions and party conflict and hatred'.

The part played by the Arminian strain of influence in developing American activism may be shown best by a review of the various reform movements which swept across the nation in the eighteen-thirties and forties. The Methodists, the Baptists, and the Disciples, after 1830, together with the New School Presbyterians and the Congregationalists, were the religious bodies leading in the temperance crusade which swept the country in the 'thirties and 'forties. The same religious bodies were also principally responsible for the reviving of the temperance movement following the Civil War; for the formation of the Anti-Saloon League and for the placing of the Eighteenth Amendment into the Federal Constitution. While the New School Presbyterians, the Congregationalists, and the Unitarians furnished the most prominent anti-slavery leadership, the Methodists and Baptists furnished the overwhelming majority of the rank and file. Even in New England, where the early abolition movement centred, and where the Congregationalists were the dominant religious body, it has been found that the majority of delegates to the anti-slavery conventions were Baptists and Methodists. Whole congregations of Methodists went over to the abolitionists and the Baptists emulated their Methodist brethren.[a] In fact, the two denominations made up the strength of the movement and more than two-thirds of all abolitionists in New England were either Baptists or Methodists. The flood of books and pamphlets dealing with the sin of slavery which appeared in the ten years preceding the Civil War were all written by men who held that since man was responsible for the introduction of slavery into America, it was his responsibility to see that this great wrong be righted.

IV

THE GERMAN STREAM OF INFLUENCE

Of the major European religious and theological currents which have influenced America the Lutheran has been the least important. One of the principal reasons for this fact is that Lutheranism came to America through the medium of non-English-speaking people, principally Germans and Scandinavians. The Swedish Lutheran Churches which were established on the Delaware in the seventeenth century were practically all absorbed by the end of the colonial period by the English-speaking Churches. The colonial Lutherans of German background, under the leadership of Henry M. Muhlenberg, had gone forward rapidly on the road to Americanization, but the Germanizing influences following his death, together with the great influx of German immigration of the 1830's and 1840's, with its emphasis upon strict conformity to all the Lutheran symbolical books, put a speedy end to the Americanizing tendencies.[b] The net result was that the Lutherans in America became Churches apart from the main currents of American life, centring their interests upon people of their own kind and background.

One of the principal reasons for the German Lutheran immigration in the 1830's and 1840's was to get away from growing rationalism in Germany. As a consequence, out of this immigration

---

[a] G. H. Barnes, *The Anti-Slavery Impulse*, pp. 90–1.
[b] Vergilius Ferm, *The Crisis in American Lutheran Theology* (New York 1927).

came a whole group of ultra-conservative Lutheran Churches, more Lutheran than Luther, of which the Missouri Synod is the most extreme example. Not only does this Church refuse to have any dealings with non-Lutheran bodies, but it stands entirely aloof from all other Lutheran Churches. The United Lutheran Church, constituted largely of the descendants of the colonial Lutherans, is the most co-operative, and the only one to have any connexion with the Federal Council of Churches, although its relationship is consultative only.

While all of the American Lutheran Churches have maintained their European character and emphasis theologically to a greater degree than any other large Protestant body, they have, however, been greatly influenced in their forms of Church government by their American environment. The Scandinavian Lutheran bodies, for instance, did not transplant their Old-World Episcopal systems, but have developed here a Congregational-Presbyterian type of polity, in which the laity have an important part. The same is true of the conservative Lutheran Churches of German background. The fact that Luther did not consider any particular form of Church government as divinely prescribed has left the American Lutheran Churches free to develop types of polity best suited to serve their particular purpose.

Of all the Protestant bodies in America the Lutheran Churches profited most from immigration. At least a third of the total German immigration since 1820 has been Lutheran, while the large Scandinavian immigration was practically a hundred per cent. Lutheran in background, though only a relatively small proportion of them in the United States are Church members. Though insulating themselves to a large degree from the common Church life in America, the people who constitute the great Lutheran bodies, both Germans and Scandinavians, have fairly generally been loyal to American democratic ideals and have made worthy contributions to all phases of American life. It is a significant fact, however, that although there have been numerous Lutheran colleges established in America, none of them have become institutions of distinction, and their student bodies are still largely limited to Lutherans. Nor has American Lutheranism made any large contribution to theological scholarship.

To quote Professor Wentz: 'Lutheranism in Europe lost its protestant character when it identified itself with the State; Lutheranism in America through a series of causes recovered its protestant character and expresses it in cultural and theological conservatism. Through much of their history in this country Lutherans have been a "conflict society" intent upon maintaining their doctrinal distinction from other groups, no matter how much they may resemble those other groups in piety and polity. So, the "spirit of isolated national ecclesiasticism" which Troeltsch ascribes to Lutheranism in Europe has its counterpart in the cultural conservatism of the Lutherans in America.'[a]

While such nineteenth-century German theologians as Schleiermacher, Ritschl, and Lotze exercised a significant influence upon American theological thought, they did so because they all represented a point of view and an emphasis which was more or less in harmony with the American trends. Ritschlianism, stressing religious experience as more fundamental than doctrine, was a dominant influence in American liberal theology for a generation, and was one of the factors in creating the Social Gospel emphasis. Schleiermacher (1768–1834) likewise found many disciples in America and he too stressed that doctrine was dependent upon religious experience, not experience on doctrine. The Lotze (1817–81) influence was brought to America largely through Borden P. Bowne, who for a generation was the bright philosophical and theological star in American Methodism. It was Lotze who helped Bowne lay the foundations for his philosophy of personalism, in which he stressed 'the immanence of God, the ethical character of religious experience', and the reality of the self. It was because of the importance which he placed upon personality that he came to designate his philosophy as 'Personalism'.

Such theological concepts as those indicated above were congenial to the American emphasis and temper, but a European theology which began to exercise large influence in America at the beginning of the depression era, was entirely out of step with the American tradition. This was known as the 'Crisis Theology', or Neo-orthodoxy, or Neo-Calvinism and Neo-Lutheranism. Now a highly developed theological system, its father was Karl Barth, a Reformed theologian in several German universities and, since his exile by the Nazis in 1935, at Basel.

The principal emphasis in this theology is the 'unbridgeable crevasse between God and man'; that man and God can have no direct relationship because God is 'totally other' than man. Every human attempt to build bridges between man and God or to bring together the divine and human is vain. Our knowledge of God comes from God and not from the religious nature of man. That God has not 'revealed Himself once and for all, but that from time to time He reveals Himself'; and 'even in the revelation of Christ no general idea of God is revealed, no valid and demonstrable idea'.[a] This all boils down to mean that man and God cannot work together to make a better world. It means the absolute rejection of the entire Social Gospel emphasis; that God alone can reform society; but God is not interested in society, His concern is to attend and assist the individual soul 'in its passage through time to eternity'. The victory of God is achieved 'not in history but beyond history', for the world is bound 'to go to pot'. Here is quietism *par excellence*; a do-nothing theology, which to the average American seems to be perfect nonsense.

This new European stress in theology came out of what seemed to be the hopeless situation in Europe after the First World War. Man had made such a sorry mess of things that he simply threw up his hands and said, in the words of the Hardshell Baptists on the American frontier: 'If God wants a better world He will bring it about in His own time and way'; a perfect Barthian phrase which was commonly heard among the most ignorant frontier Baptists more than a hundred years ago.

Barthianism came to America through two influences. One was through some exceedingly able young American theologians of recent European background and training. Of these Reinhold Niebuhr and Paul Tillich are the best known. A second influence was the reaction against the extreme humanism which had gained widespread acceptance among Liberals in America, with its antitheistic and anti-supernatural emphasis. But even at the time of its greatest vogue, during the period of lush times of the 'twenties, it failed to win the vast body of moderately Liberal opinion. The extremely radical wing of this humanistic theology had watered God down to man's size and had more or less bowed Him out of the universe. It was a fair-weather theology and flourished when times were good, but, with the coming of hard times during the deep depression years, a different kind of God other than the 'human will to goodness' was demanded. Thus the soil was made

[a] Adolf Keller, *Religion and the European Mind* (London 1934); especially Chapter 3, pp. 45–69.

ready for the Barthian emphasis upon a transcendent God, which led to the ready acceptance of semi-Barthian views among many former Liberals.

As already indicated, one of the effects of this influence in America has been the discrediting of the Social Gospel, though within recent years there is a definite reaction, and an increasing number of unrepentant Liberals have been reasserting the Liberal faith that is still in them.

V

THE SOCIAL GOSPEL EMPHASIS IN AMERICAN PROTESTANTISM

Those who have attempted to trace the origins of the Social Gospel emphasis in American Protestantism, which has been characterized as the most unique contribution that America has made to the stream of ongoing Christianity, have thought of it as having arisen in the period of rapid industrial change which began in the years immediately following the Civil War. But the roots of the Social Gospel are to be found in the very nature of American Protestantism itself. In other words the Social Gospel is definitely in the stream of American religious development, which rises in left-wing Protestantism; derives from the frontier emphasis and revivalism; and has been fed by the Calvinistic and Arminian tributaries.[a] The generation following the Civil War witnessed rapid transformation in all phases of American life. In the realm of business these years saw the rise of the great corporations, which by 1919 were employing eighty-six per cent. of the wage-earners, and were producing more than eighty-seven per cent. of the total value of products. These years also saw the beginning of the organized labour movement, in the formation of the Knights of Labor in 1869, and in the organization of the American Federation of Labor in 1881. At the same time the United States was rapidly changing from a predominantly rural to an urban society through the movement of population into the great industrial centres. The astonishing growth of American cities which was a concomitant of the social and economic revolution was not only due to the influx of population from small towns and rural areas to meet the demands of industry, but also

[a] W. A. Visser t' Hooft. *The Background of the Social Gospel in America* (Haarlem 1928) pp. 1–14. Charles Howard Hopkins, *The Rise of the Social Gospel in American Protestantism, 1865–1915* (New Haven 1940), pp. 11–13.

to the vast immigration from northern Europe, in the years immediately following the war, and after 1880 from southern and eastern Europe.[a]

During the very years in which these revolutionary changes were in process in the economic and social life of the nation, the great evangelical Churches, which had met with reasonable adequacy the problems posed by population movements westward, were themselves undergoing economic and social transformation. Many of the men who were the leaders in the creation of the great business corporations, and had amassed vast fortunes as a result, were staunch Churchmen. John D. Rockefeller and Cyrus H. McCormick are but examples of numerous others. Men of wealth began to make princely gifts to religious and educational foundations and more and more attained leadership in the councils of their respective Churches. Membership in the large Protestant Churches came to be made up more and more of employers, salaried persons, farmers, and those engaged in personal service for capitalists. The Churches, such as the Baptists, the Methodists, and the Disciples, formerly proud to call themselves the Churches of the poor, now boasted of their great endowments and the number of millionaires in their membership. Thus the changes taking place in American Protestantism during these years, instead of conditioning the Churches to deal with the social and economic changes in the nation, were, in fact, setting up barriers which made adjustment to the new conditions difficult.

The prevailing theological atmosphere of the time was conservative, though the hard and over-emotionalized religion which had characterized the frontier stage of our religious development was gradually giving way to a more easy-going religion, a type of religion which finds a large acceptance among well-to-do people, who generally want only enough religion to be accounted respectable, but not enough to be bothersome. These are the kind of people who often keep their religion in an airtight compartment and who insist that business is business and politics is politics, and neither have anything to do with religion.

The social and economic unrest which followed upon the heels of the Civil War broke in upon this complacent religion with explosive results. The latter 'seventies and the 'eighties was a

---

[a] A. M. Schlesinger, 'The Rise of the City, 1878–98' (Vol. X, *A History of American Life*) (New York 1933).

period of industrial strife throughout the United States. During the year 1886 alone there were nearly 1,600 separate labour disturbances which involved 600,000 men and a financial loss of $34,000,000. In 1892 came the great steel strike in Pittsburg, caused by the sharp reduction in wages and the refusal of the corporation to recognize the Steel Workers Union. Two years later the most disastrous of the strikes of the period was precipitated among the employees of the Pullman Car Company in Chicago which eventually involved all the railroads entering Chicago. These violent disturbances, instead of elicitating Church support for better wages and living conditions for labour, blinded them to the injustices against which labour was in revolt. Indeed, the Church papers of the time generally voiced anti-labour sentiments. The vast waste and destruction involved in the strikes seemed to Church people as wicked, a violation of their Puritan notion of thrift, and they blamed labour rather than capital for the loss.

As a result of this unsympathetic attitude of the Churches toward labour there was developing clearly discernible cleavages between labour and the Church. This began to cause concern on the part of an increasing number of thoughtful men who were slowly coming to a different point of view, and who were determined to do something about it. At the same time the new study of sociology began to find a place in the colleges and universities, and a group of economists 'with religious presuppositions' were calling attention to the dangers to American society which the growing tension between capital and labour was creating.

The names most intimately connected with the early phase of the movement in American Protestantism which soon became known as the Social Gospel were Washington Gladden, a Congregational minister in Columbus, Ohio, Professor Francis G. Peabody, Professor of Social Ethics in Harvard University, and groups at the new University of Chicago, headed by Charles R. Henderson and Shailer Mathews. Leading economists in the universities such as John R. Commons and Richard T. Ely were not only in sympathy with the emphasis in religion but were in hearty co-operation with the ministers who were advancing it. The man, however, who meant more for the movement than any other was Walter Rauschenbusch, who has been characterized as 'social Christianity's greatest prophet'.

The movement from the start was no fly-by-night affair, for

from its beginning those who agitated Christianity's concern for the social order based their agitation on a thorough study of the conditions which had produced the crisis. They all agreed with the economist John R. Commons that not only do Christian people need the heart of love, 'but also the knowledge to guide their love', and they were busy acquiring that knowledge. The result was an impressive list of books and innumerable articles in papers and magazines proclaiming the new Gospel. Josiah Strong, Washington Gladden, Shailer Mathews, Henry C. King, and numerous others made notable contributions, but 'the classic statement of American social Christianity is that of Walter Rauschenbusch', found in his *Christianity and the Social Crisis* (1907); *Christianizing the Social Order* (1912); and the *Theology of the Social Gospel* (1917).[a]

This movement to put religion to work to reform the social order met opposition from the beginning from at least three sources. As was to be expected, big business opposed it, and the movement found hard sledding in the Churches of the upper-classes. It also met opposition from those bodies which were still stressing the revivalistic emphasis. They considered the chief business of the Church to deliver individuals from sin and spiritual death; they contended that the only way to reform society and to make the social order Christian was to win individuals to the Christian way of life. As was to be expected opposition also came from the quietistic Churches, particularly those of Lutheran and German background, which had carried over the European view that the world for the most part must learn to shift for itself. However, the movement gained momentum in the great evangelical Churches, especially among the Methodists, Baptists, Congregationalists, Presbyterians, and Disciples, all of whom have not only adopted social creeds but established organizations to put those social creeds into practice.

The ruling ideas which underlay the Social Gospel were first of all the *immanence of God*, the possibility of the union of the heavenly and the earthly; secondly, the vital unity of the race implied in the doctrine of the fatherhood of God and the brotherhood of man which called for a brotherhood 'supreme over all inequalities and diversities, and that no man lives or dies or attains happiness apart from his fellow men'. Thirdly, that

---

[a] The most adequate treatment of the Social Gospel movement in American Protestantism is that of Charles Howard Hopkins, *The Rise of the Social Gospel in American Protestantism, 1865–1915* (New Haven, Yale University Press, 1940).

salvation meant not only the restoration of man to a state of purity, it meant also the creating of a new humanity in Christ. 'Obedience to the first commandment saves the individual, observance to the second saves society.' All of these conceptions added up to the possibility of establishing the kingdom of heaven on earth.

The hope of the possibility of establishing the kingdom of God on earth suffered a tremendous setback in America as a result of the First World War and the depression. The coming of the Second World War and the vast confusion and human suffering attending its aftermath, seemed to discredit completely the whole Social Gospel emphasis. Many Social Gospellers in the face of these tragic facts lost their enthusiasm and began to turn more and more to the pessimistic theology coming out of Europe, which stressed man's impotence and inability to do anything to transform the world. Such a theology, however, is not at home even in a confused and groping America. And God pity us and the world if the time ever comes when we shall throw all the burden on the Lord and fold the hands and acquiesce.

INDEX

ACTIVISM, 54–74
Alleghenies, 14
America, discovery of, 1
American Federation of Labour, 70
Anabaptists, 19
Anglicans, 7
Anne, Queen, 5
Anti-Catholic Movements, 49
   -Saloon League, 35, 65
   -Slavery Movement, 59 n., 60, 62
Armenians, 47
Arminianism, 64, 70
Asbury, F., 17 f., 55
Assemblies, 33
Awakenings, 8

BAINTON, R. H., 3 n.
Baptists, 3, 7, 11, 15, 21, 26, 30, 32 f., 36
   39, 48, 64 ff., 69, 71, 73
Barnes, A., 62
   G. H., 59 n., 62 f. n., 66 n.
Barth, K., 68 f.
Bates, E. S., 3 n.
Batten, J. M., 2 n.
Becker, C., 35
Beecher, L., 62
Bellamy, J., 59
Bennett, J. S., 26 n.
Bible, 23 f., 60
   Society, 35
Billington, R. A., 49 n.
Bishops, 6
Bloomington, Ind., 20
Boston, 30, 47
Bourne, H. R. F., 10 n.
Bowne, B. P., 68
Brooks, P., 64
Buckham, J. W., 63 n.
Bulgarians, 47
Burke, E., 9

CADDEN, J. P., 46 n.
Calhoun, J. C., 61
Calvin, J., 2, 3
Calvinism, 7, 55, 58, 60, 64, 70
Camp-Meetings, 23, 35
Carolinas, 6
Carroll, C., 45
   J., 50
Cartwright, P., 21
Carver, G. W., 43
Catechism, 23
Chautauqua, 24, 35
Chicago, 36, 48, 72
Christendom, 37

Christian Century, 37
   Herald, 37
Church History, 37
   Union, 35, 37
Churches of God, 33
Civil War, 26, 39, 65 f., 70 f.
Coke, T., 18
Colleges, 36, 41
Commons, J. R., 72
Communism, 51 f.
Confessional Churches, 1
Confirmation, 7
Congregationalists, 3, 7, 15, 17, 24 ff.,
   30, 36, 62, 65
Congress, 21
Cranmer, T., 2
Crisis-Theology, 68
Cumberland Presbyterian Church, 33
Cunningham, C. E., 60 n.
Czechs, 47

DELAWARE, 66
Democratic Party, 64
Denominations, U.S.A., 28 ff.
Disciples, 17, 24, 32, 36, 64 f., 71, 73
Dunaway, W. F., 5 n.
Dunkers, 5
Dutch Reformed Church, 15
Dwight, T., 60 f.

EDUCATION, 26, 36, 41, 60 f.
Edward VI, Prayer Books of, 2
Edwards, J., 7, 25, 59 ff., 64 f.
Ely, R. T., 72
England, Church of, 2
   J., 50
Episcopalians, 15, 17
Eucken, R., 55

FAIRCHILD, J. H., 63 n.
Ferm, V., 66 n.
Finney, C. G., 26, 59 f., 62
Foreign Missions, 35, 60
Franco, 51
Frontier, 31
Froude, J. A., 6

GALLATIN, A., 9
Garrison, W. E., 51
   W. L., 62
Georgia, 6
Germans, 4 f., 47, 66, 73
Germany, 1
Gewehr, W. M., 8 n.
Gibbons, Cardinal, 50

Gladden, W., 64, 72 f.
Gordon, G. A., 64
Greeks, 47
Guilday, P., 46 n.
Gypsy Smith, 25

HALLE, 5
Harrington, E. T., 46 f. n.
Harvard Divinity School, 36
  Theological Review, 37
Hayes, C. J. H., 3 n.
Henderson, C. R., 72
Herrnhut, 5
Hirsch, A. H., 4 n.
Hocking, W. E., 55
Home Missions, 35
Hooft, W. A. V. t', 12 n., 70 n.
Hooker, T., 57
Hopkins, C. H., 70 n., 73 n.
Hughes, J., 50
Huguenots, 4
Humphrey, E. F., 9 n.
Hungarians, 47

IMMIGRATION, 4 f., 46
Independents, 19
Indians, 43
Ireland, J., 50
Irish, 46 f.
Italians, 48

JEFFERSON, T., 11, 64
Jews, 28, 48, 50
Journal of Religion, 37

KELLER, A., 69 n.
Kentucky, 21, 23
King, H. C., 73
Kipling, R., 54 f.
Knights of Labour, 70
Ku-Klux-Klan, 52

LATVIANS, 47
LeFarge, J., 50 n.
Left-wing Churches, 1 f., 11
Leo XIII, 50
Lewis, J., 18 n.
Lincoln, A., 21
Lindsay, T. M., 2
Lithuanians, 47
Locke, J., 10, 29
Logan, R. W., 44 n.
Lord, R. H., 46 f. n.
Lotze, H., 68
Luther, M., 2 f.
Lutheran Churches, 1, 15, 17, 36, 66 f., 73

MADISON, J., 11, 29 f.
Maine, 5
Maryland, 3 f.

Mascall, R., 3 n.
Matthews, S., 72
Maxson, C. H., 8 n.
Maynard, T., 45 n., 47 n.
Mays, B. E., 41 f. n.
McCormick, C. H., 71
McGiffert, A. C., 59 n.
McGready, J., 23
Mead, S. E., 61 n.
Mecklin, J. M., 10 n., 49 n.
Membership, Church, 6, 28, 33 ff., 39, 46
Mennonites, 5
Methodist Episcopal Church, South, 40
Methodists, 8, 15–21, 23–6, 32 f., 36 f., 39, 48, 64 ff., 71, 73
Mexicans, 48
Miller, P., 54 n., 57 f. n.
Mississippi, River, 14
Missouri, State of, 47, 67
Mode, P. G., 26 n.
Moody, D. L., 25
Moravians, 5
Mormons, 32
Muhlenberg, H. M., 5, 66
Munger, T. T., 64

NAZARINE, CHURCH OF, 33
Nazis, 56, 68
Negro Churches, 33 f., 39 ff.
  Colleges, 41
  Negroes, 39–44
New England, 3, 11, 30, 47, 57 f.
  Haven, 61
  York, 3 f., 28
Newman, J. H., 50
Nicaea, Council of, 2, 38
Nicholson, J. W., 41 f. n.
Niebuhr, H. Reinhold, 69
  H. Richard, 31, 57 n.
Niemoeller, Pastor, 56

OBERLIN COLLEGE, 26, 59
Orthodox, Eastern, 28

PAUL, ST., 57
Peabody, F. G., 72
Penn, W., 6
Pharaoh, 43
Pietists, 5, 7
Pilgrim Holiness Church, 33
Pius IX, 50
Poles, 47 f.
Population, 4
Portuguese, 48
Presbyterian Church, 1, 15 f., 21, 23 f., 26, 36, 48, 62, 65, 73
Princeton, Ill., 20
Protestantism, 1–4, 26 ff., 37 f., 48, 50 ff. 70 f.
Puritans, 20, 57 f.

QUAKERS, 4, 15, 18 f.

RALL, H. F., 55 n., 57 n.
Rauschenbusch, W., 72 f.
Ray, M. A., 45 n.
Reformation, 1
Reformed Churches, 1, 35
Religion in Life, 37
Revivals, 7 f., 22 ff.
Revolution, American, 9
Rhode Island, 3
Right-wing Churches, 1 f.
Ritschl, A., 68
Rockefeller, J. D., 71
Roman Catholics, 11, 15, 28, 30 f.,
  45–53
Russians, 47, 51, 53

SABBATH, 13 f.
Scandinavians, 1, 35, 47, 66 f.
Schleiermacher, F., 68
Schlesinger, A. M., 71 n.
Schneider, C. E., 56 n.
Schwenkfelders, 5
Scotch-Irish, 5
Scotland, 1
Seminaries, 36
Sexton, J. E., 46 f. n.
Shaughnessy, G., 46
Slaves, slavery, 34, 39 f.
Slovaks, 47
Smith, Al., 51
  Joseph, 32
Smyth, N., 64
Spellman, Cardinal, 50
Sperry, W. L., 42 n., 50 n., 54
'Spirituals', 42
State Churches, 12, 15
Stillingfleet, E., 10
Stone, B. W., 24
Stowe, H. B., 63
Strickland, R. C., 6 n.
Strikes, 72
Strong, J., 73
Sunday School Union, 35
  W., 25

Sweet, W. W., 3 n., 5 n., 7 n., 11 n.,
  13 f. n., 18 n., 22 n., 24 n., 26 f. n.
  37 n., 41 n., 46 n.
Switzerland, 1

TAYLOR, N. W., 59, 61
Temperance, 35, 65
Tennent, G., 25
Test Act, 1704, 6
Tewkesbury, D. G., 26 n.
Thornwell, J. H., 40 n.
Tiffin, E., 21
Tillich, P., 69
Tipple, E. S., 18
Toleration, 29
Tories, 6
Tract Society, 35
Troeltsch, E., 12, 58, 68
Turner, F. J., 61 n.
Tyrconnell, 6

UKRAINIANS, 47
'Uncle Tomism', 44
Uniat Church, 48
Union Theological Seminary, 36
Unitarianism, 33, 64 f.
Universalism, 33, 64
Universities, 36, 41, 46

WEBER, M., 58
Weld, T. D., 62
Wentz, A. R., 67 f.
Wesley, J., 7, 17, 65
Westminster Confession, 3, 20
Whitefield, G., 8
Williams, R., 10
Wisconsin, 47
Wittke, C., 4 n.
Woodson, C. G., 41 n.

YALE COLLEGE, 60 f.
  Divinity School, 36
Y.M.C.A., 27
Y.W.C.A., 27

ZWINGLI, H., 2

Printed in Great Britain by
The Camelot Press Ltd., London and Southampton